BON

The L. Ron Hubbard Series

Bridge Publications, Inc.
5600 E. Olympic Blvd.
Commerce, California 90022 USA

ISBN 978-1-4031-9889-1

Special acknowledgment is made to the L. Ron Hubbard Library for permission to reproduce photographs from his personal collection. Additional credits: pp. 1, 7, 29, 67, 85, 103, back cover Dman/Shutterstock.com; pp. 19, 22, 25, 38, 55, 58, 73 kanate/Shutterstock.com; p. 8 Hulton Archive/Getty Images; p. 10 Craig Hanson/Shutterstock.com; p. 11 National Archives; p. 13 Michael Ochs Archives/Getty Images; p. 14 Jim Daly Photography Studio; p. 29 SuperStock/Getty Images; p. 66 Jay M. Pasachoff/Getty Images; p. 68 Library of Congress Prints and Photographs, Division Washington, DC; pp. 74, 81 Derek R. Audette/Shutterstock.com.

Printed in the United States of America

The L. Ron Hubbard Series: Restoring Honor & Self-Respect—English

The L. Ron Hubbard Series

HUMANITARIAN
RESTORING
HONOR &
SELF-RESPECT

Bridge

PUBLICATIONS, INC.®

CONTENTS

An Introduction to
L. Ron Hubbard

"WE HAVE THE ANSWERS TO HUMAN SUFFERING," L. Ron Hubbard very truthfully declared, "and they are available to everyone." In particular, he spoke of a means to replace intolerance with kindness, criminality with decency, degradation with dignity and honor. In short, he spoke of all that is made possible with his tools for personal ethics and his nonreligious moral code, *The Way to Happiness,* and thus all he himself stood for as our most relevant humanitarian.

As the Founder of Dianetics and Scientology, there is no quarter of society L. Ron Hubbard's work is not felt. For with those subjects come truths that embrace all existence. Yet given the sheer numbers touched by his writings on ideal human conduct—literally tens of millions—one simply cannot discuss modern ethics and morality without reference to LRH.

How Ron came to address these matters and the worldwide impact of his discoveries is, of course, the subject of this publication. Nevertheless, certain fundamentals must be understood from the outset. In the first place, when we speak of what LRH brought to the field of ethics, we are speaking of an Ethics *Technology,* a complete system for ethical improvement. At the heart of that system is an encompassing view of ethics as rationality toward the highest level of survival for *all* things. Thus ethics becomes not an abstract, but a functional tool by which we ensure prosperity, happiness and survival along every avenue of existence.

How those tools are utilized involves another LRH revelation—this concerning the various ethical states or conditions that determine how successfully one survives. That is, one may be surviving more or less well according to one's degree of ethical conduct, but much improvement is still possible. Consequently we find what LRH defined as the Conditions of Existence and his step-by-step formulas by which those conditions may be bettered.

The resounding point: With LRH technology, ethics is no longer a contemplative

"I will not admit that there is a naturally bad, evil man on Earth" —L. Ron Hubbard

subject for obtuse debate on right or wrong. It is a living, breathing force for good, with real application to every aspect of our lives.

philosophy to the bedrock of postindustrial despair. En route, we alternately find Ron facing crews of veritable cutthroats in the North

"We have the answers to human suffering and they are available to everyone."

Likewise, with *The Way to Happiness,* "morality" is no longer another buzzword for political aspirants and talk-radio hosts. It is a weapon with which to combat all that plagues a twenty-first century on the rim of a moral abyss, including: urban mayhem, domestic infidelity, corporate rapacity, political malfeasance and even international conflict. Then, too, with L. Ron Hubbard's *The Way to Happiness* comes the singular answer to all criminality and prison populations of epic proportions (millions in the United States alone).

Unquestionably, then, this road to restored honor and self-respect, as paved by LRH discoveries, is a vastly important one. It also happens to be an entirely fascinating road, winding from the pinnacle of Western

Atlantic, conducting advanced sociological studies in lower Manhattan and walking an especially murderous beat as a Special Officer for the Los Angeles Police Department. Needless to say, we also find a supremely compassionate L. Ron Hubbard who continued to maintain that if some men may indeed pose a menace to society, "I will not admit that there is a naturally bad, evil man on Earth."

Nevertheless, and as Ron so rightly predicted, this world has indeed seen an ethical and moral crisis of monstrous dimensions—first in the shape of soaring crime rates and commensurately escalating law enforcement, then in a monolithic prison system incarcerating more men and women than any society has ever imprisoned in the name of crime control. (To cite another telling statistic: in the space of barely ten years, the state of California built twenty-one new prisons, while a single New York county spawned another five facilities in just over the same span.)

Meanwhile, among those statistically ripe for the cells are the 20 percent of all teenage students packing weapons in classrooms and the 50 percent of all American high-school students who freely admit they would lie, cheat, pad expense accounts or otherwise profit illicitly if the gains outweighed the risks. In consequence to the latter, of course, is all this world has witnessed in the way of corporate looting, insider dealing and public distrust to the very pinnacle of political power. While just to cap it: with some fifty or so billion annual dollars spent on American correctional facilities to house inmates totaling the combined populations of Atlanta, Denver, New Orleans, St. Louis and Miami, and with better than half of those prisoners rearrested within three years of release, one logically has to ask: perhaps there's something lacking in this realm of ethics, justice and morality?

The official reply has been vociferous but largely pointless: political referendums for the reinstatement of a moral curriculum in our schools (however undefined), harsher penalties for white-collar crime, mandatory jail time for dozens of other crimes and erecting still more prisons. While to justify their own place in this big-money criminal-justice system, psychologists and psychiatrists have fobbed off a whole new array of phrases, including: *chromosomal violence tendency, sociopathic disorder* and—however inherently racist—*genetic inclination to violence.* As we shall see, such thinking is not only irrelevant, it's part of the problem and why it becomes so utterly significant when L. Ron Hubbard speaks of this road to honor and self-respect in terms of returning to Man "some of the happiness, some of the sincerity and some of the love and kindness with which he was created." ∎

CHAPTER ONE

Finding the Road
TO SELF-RESPECT

Finding the Road
to Self-Respect

THERE IS NOT A CRIMINAL IN THE WORLD, L. RON HUBBARD tells us, whose life of crime cannot be traced to a loss of self-respect. And if we were to ask that criminal what is meant by a loss of self-respect, we would inevitably hear the most pitiful phrase imaginable: "One day I found I couldn't trust myself."

How Ron came to recognize the import of that statement and its greater implications as regards the whole of crime and punishment is a fairly vast story. For when speaking of criminality and the loss of self-respect, he explains, one is speaking of a spiritual being who has ultimately betrayed his own essence, who has broken the one contract he must not break: *the contract with himself.*

As an entrance into that realm, however, as a preliminary word, so to speak, he points to a seemingly insignificant incident from the summer of 1926. The details are these: Having signed on with Montana state rangers to help cut fire trails, the then fifteen-year-old Ron soon found himself working with a number of young men late from the state penitentiary at Joliet, Illinois. Consequently, as he put

it, one encountered all sorts of interesting complications. Yet surprisingly or not, actual viciousness was rare. Nor, he concluded, did one find an absence of integrity, as underscored by the convict who drove two hundred miles in a *stolen* vehicle to return Ron a pair of borrowed boots. But in either case, he added, those of the criminal society "have strange ways of transacting business in life."

The next incident of note—and this one proved key—came in 1935. The previous year had seen the sale of Ron's first short stories to New York publishers and his entrance into the ranks of American popular fiction. Although best known for his tales of high adventure, he also supplied westerns, romances and a number of exceedingly well-wrought detective

Washington, DC, 1924: the distinguished Boy Scout who would soon supervise teams of young delinquents cutting fire trails in the Montana wilderness

yarns. Through the course of research for the latter, he eventually interviewed a host of law enforcement professionals, including police officers, coroners and federal investigators. But plainly most unforgettable was his tour, with fellow author Arthur J. Burks, of the New York State penitentiary of Sing Sing.

His impressions are recorded in several places, but most notably in a 1938 unpublished manuscript entitled "Excalibur." The first delineation of discoveries that led directly to Dianetics, "Excalibur" stands as the original explanation of Survive as the common denominator of all life. That is, however varied was behavior from one life form to another, all life ultimately sought only to survive. (Hence his later view of ethics as rationality towards the highest level of survival for all things.) But extrapolating from that central revelation are chapters on how the urge towards survival is reflected in government, finance, education, the arts and criminal reform... And through his discussion of the latter, he offers a chilling indictment of life and death in Sing Sing.

In the first place, he writes, the prison reforms nothing, and all one learns in a cage is that he has indeed become an animal. In the second place, prison in no way constitutes justice. And, in fact, "There is no man upon this Earth with mind enough to dispense justice." Finally, and this in response to a thorough inspection of the electric chair: "The life of each and every man belongs to himself and himself alone. His days on Earth are few, his happiness limited. Against him are all the counts of disease, starvation, failure in business, wrecks, deaths of friends and half a million more.

"To this the state has no right or power to add revenge and call it JUSTICE."

To then drive the point home, he supplies an immensely powerful account of an execution beginning with the placement of the copper cap upon the shaved head and concluding with the attendant physician's workaday pronouncement, "Okay, he's stiff." Included among the details: The condemned will invariably glimpse the autopsy tables (concaved to receive the blood) and the coffin where his body will rest. The executioner receives three hundred dollars for the killing but must see to the maintenance of machinery. The force of the jolt quite often snaps the chest strap while the juice continues flowing for as long as twenty minutes. In what amounted to an addendum, he noted in a later conversation, the experience had left him quite repulsed: "We didn't feel like doing anything for about a week" and then

elsewhere concluded imprisonment to be quite antithetical to rehabilitation. Rather, "It breaks men; it finishes them!"

For some time thereafter, he spoke of these matters only sporadically, as in a revised note for the "Excalibur" manuscript: A man is not necessarily a menace to society simply because he commits a crime. "He becomes a menace only when he has to compensate with dangerousness for his own loss of prestige." By late 1942, however, his ideas on crime and punishment had already begun to assume a workable methodology.

Again the circumstances require a word of explanation. Having entered the United States Navy in 1941 and seen hard action in the South Pacific, now Lieutenant Hubbard returned to American waters to assume command of a battle-ready corvette providing a measure of resistance to what had become a devastating U-boat menace. Yet so ill-equipped were the vessels of this

Left
Portland, Oregon, 1943: given an acute shortage of able seamen, then Lieutenant L. Ron Hubbard enlisted recalcitrant sailors from a naval brig and transformed them into crack combat crews

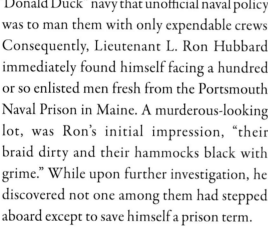
"Donald Duck" navy that unofficial naval policy was to man them with only expendable crews. Consequently, Lieutenant L. Ron Hubbard immediately found himself facing a hundred or so enlisted men fresh from the Portsmouth Naval Prison in Maine. A murderous-looking lot, was Ron's initial impression, "their braid dirty and their hammocks black with grime." While upon further investigation, he discovered not one among them had stepped aboard except to save himself a prison term.

Yet as a first order of business, Ron ceremoniously dispensed with their service records—literally dumped them into a mail sack and deposited the sack in a safe. He then explained that with the commencement of duties aboard his vessel all slates were clean, all past crimes immaterial. On the other hand, he made it clear his word was law and no dereliction would be tolerated. That is, since the survival of all depended upon the performance of all, then exemplary service was expected from each and every man. Then followed a period of thoroughly rigorous drilling until, as Ron quipped, "These men were standing *sea watches* in undress blues merely because they thought it would look better."

He drew no summary conclusion beyond the fact that, with a measure of pride and the weight of "super officialdom and dossiers off their back," these men had been transformed from criminals to seamen in the space of about six weeks. Moreover, they were superb seamen with some seventy depth-charge runs to their credit and not a single casualty. But the larger questions of criminality and the particulars of rehabilitation—these matters were yet to be resolved.

In a simple statement of the question now at hand, he was to explain: "I was trying to find out if criminal minds were different kinds of minds" and, by corollary, what then constituted "police minds." Yet to appreciate that question, one must appreciate where the longer road to the development of Dianetics had thus far taken him.

As of early 1947, the fundamental techniques of Dianetics were in place. That which we now know as the ultimate source of human aberration, criminal or otherwise, was very nearly in sight and procedures for the restoration of sanity, happiness and the alleviation of psychosomatic ills were at hand. Also established was what he described as the inherent goodness of the basic personality. In other words—and this from LRH himself—however deranged the behavior, the core personality was found to be "strong, hardy and constructively good!"

The ramifications of that statement were, of course, immense—particularly in light of a pervasive psychological theory that held Man to be the product of his evolutionary heritage, i.e., the

upright and thinking killer. Then too, Ron was not speaking in any theoretical sense. But rather, having utilized early Dianetics techniques on some several hundred cases, he had ultimately found that even beneath the so-called hardened criminal lay "a sincere, intelligent being with ambition and cooperativeness." Or more simply: "Man was basically good. Social nature was inherent!" There still remained, however, that question of what precipitated criminal behavior—what

comprised its common denominator, as LRH phrased it—and to resolve that matter, he commenced an examination of the criminal realm as a Special Officer for the Los Angeles Police Department.

An outgrowth of the greater urban sprawl, leaving the city with roughly half the officers per capita as New York or Chicago, the Los Angeles Special Officer had become a fairly common sight as of 1948. In all, some forty-five private patrols were then active across Los Angeles, most enlisted by business communities through larger detective agencies. Their primary duties were of two kinds: the guarding of particular properties, e.g., banks and warehouses, and the patrolling of a general neighborhood on behalf of local merchants.

In the latter, the Special Officer's duties were virtually the same as the regular officer, although he had no powers of arrest beyond the "citizen's arrest." He was, however, uniformed—slate gray but otherwise indistinguishable from LAPD blues—and he was armed.

It was January 1948 when Ron commenced his duties as a Special Officer. Although his employer of record was the Metropolitan Detective Agency, his ultimate license came from LAPD; for only the department possessed the authority to determine who was "fit and proper" to serve. Nor was that authority in any way a rubber stamp, for as Los Angeles Police Chief W. H. Parker had declared, "You can't be too tough when you give a man a badge and allow him to carry a gun!" Moreover, no Los Angeles police officer could walk a more challenging beat, i.e., the notorious Central Division in what is still the city's dark heart.

Encompassing about seventeen square miles beyond First and Main Streets (wherein lived but 13 percent of the city's population), the Central Division generated nearly a third of all Los Angeles crime. That is, from less than one twenty-fifth of Los Angeles came roughly 30 percent of all burglaries, robberies, murders and assaults. Causes were complex, but obviously included a large transient population—the area was littered with one-night flophouses—and a certain degree of racial tension. In particular, Central Division lay between a growing Hispanic community and the northwestern perimeter of the African-American. There was also, of course, much in the way of gang violence and that which had no real explanation at all.

Ron offers several pointed anecdotes to underscore the desolation: An intoxicated Native American threatens to kill the occupants of a Main Street bar for failing to serve him a drink. (The man is only mollified when LRH sits him down and convinces him a shot glass of water was the smoothest vodka in the civilized world.) Determined to resolve a quarrel with a friend, an equally intoxicated Alvarado Street resident attempts to snatch Ron's side arm from the holster. That LRH never actually bothered to load

the weapon was immaterial ("The cartridges are heavy," he quipped). The poor wretch perceived he had been wronged and wanted revenge, and only after what amounts to a heart-to-heart talk with Special Officer Hubbard does the offender finally conclude

one did not shoot one's friends. On the other hand, Ron observed, there is all LAPD police officers dished out in the name of law

Concurrently, however, and at every conceivable opportunity, he continued to utilize the techniques of Dianetics to search out

"...if one sincerely hopes to rehabilitate a criminal population...then this is the factor one must consider: 'Where did they lose their self-respect?'"

Below
St. Joseph's Hospital, Savannah, Georgia: site of pivotal LRH work with the criminally insane

enforcement, including billy-club beatings and forced confessions, inevitably driving petty offenders to increasingly more serious crime.... Until, as LRH so descriptively put it, life on these streets became "completely lost from all creation."

an answer. His working theory was axiomatic. If Dianetics could now be defined as "a very exact analytical approach to problems of the mind," then it could also be counted upon to provide a solution to what one might term the "criminal mind." And from that premise came a series of therapeutic tests actually conducted on those Main Street residents. Preliminary results were intriguing; for notwithstanding apparent correlations between the abused child and later delinquency, the criminal's common denominator lay not in what was *done* to the child, but rather what the child *did*. By way of example (and almost certainly drawn directly from research), he tells of a youth who very nearly bashes in the head of a sibling, at which point the critical thought became: "I could actually sink low enough to hurt my own sister." And *that,* as Ron so succinctly concluded, "is enough."

Thereafter, he explains, one is looking at an individual who has indeed abrogated a sacred contract with himself—to be ethical, decent and respectable—and therein lay the critical point of decline.

For the next several months, and continuing in Savannah, Georgia, where he worked with the criminally insane inmates of the state institution, this matter of the criminal common denominator became a definite point of study. In an especially evocative description of work through this period, he spoke of searching out that sad turning point in every life of crime, following a "long, long track" to the critical crossroad where the criminal first lost faith in himself as a decent and honorable person. Because the moment a man loses that pride of goodness and sense of honor, he explained, "It doesn't matter what he does to anyone, including himself."

As we shall see, he would eventually have much more to say on the subject—on the futility of imprisonment, the barbarity of capital punishment and a psychological interpretation of violent behavior that inevitably translates into police states. But the central realization from these days—the primary latchkey to the resolution of crime—that would remain firm: if one sincerely hopes to rehabilitate a criminal population, he concluded, then this is the factor one must consider: "Where did they lose their self-respect?" ■

Left
Bay Head, New Jersey, 1950: at birthplace of *Dianetics: The Modern Science of Mental Health*

Without high-school diplomas and either wholly or functionally illiterate, those typically occupying United States federal prison cells are indeed what L. Ron Hubbard writes of here: students attending the only college that will have them. Moreover, they typically remain faithful alumni—which accounts for America's "revolving door" prison system wherein the better part of every "graduating class" returns within three or four years for "graduate studies." Meaning: they're rearrested to serve even harder time. Hence L. Ron Hubbard's observation: "The effect of punishment on a criminal is to confirm that behavior, and cause him to insist upon it." And hence his "The Criminal College" in emphasis of the fact that twenty-first-century recidivism follows from a long and slow failure of the twentieth-century criminal reform. Indeed, the article dates from 1937 and so comprises a root discussion on the evolution of prisons, where inmates are as thoroughly stamped with the imprint of their "college" as any Ivy League alumnus. While upon graduation, and regardless of his particular major, the ex-con is just as prepared "to prove himself worthy of the only fraternity which ever took any interest in him."

THE CRIMINAL COLLEGE

by L. RON HUBBARD

THROUGHOUT THIS WIDE LAND, wherever one turns, great piles of sullen stone crouch like traps of some giant's hewing. But no trap ever possessed as many guardians and certainly no trap ever occasioned as much oratory as is yearly bleated about prisons.

One of society's most barbaric survivals, one of the sorriest comments upon the mass of humanity, the prison has been with us since the time the first Eoanthropic chieftain heaved a disorderly dawn man into a damp and inky cave.

Since that time the routine has varied little, enlivened perhaps in this age and that with the addition of torture, but always known by a few unchanging essentials.

Any man carries with him his idea of a prison, defining it as a small, poorly lighted cell wherein a person may be restrained from associating with the rest of society.

Considering the very many ways of accomplishing the fact without resorting to that exact means, and considering also that this small, dark cell remains universally basic, it is strange that no one has tried to arrive at the fundamental fact.

That fact has always been with us. Perhaps that Eoanthropic chieftain knew, but between his time and ours it is to be doubted that the crude truth has been set down.

And that truth is crude, perhaps, to our Calvinistic society. It would very likely offend many minds which care more for the conventions than for either truth or the general good.

But it can be very simply stated. And perhaps because it is so very simple, great psychiatrists and criminologists have cared to overlook it.

The sentencing of a man to prison is the combined wish of society that that man be returned to the womb from which he came. It is the mass regret that that man was ever born.

And as long as society indicates that desire, the courts and officers of the law will continue to obey the rule of the multitude and wish, in very serious forms with a very pompous air, that same fact.

"You are hereby sentenced…" might well be translated into "You should never have existed in the first place."

In the enlightened barbarism of our times, there are those with wit enough to see the stupid fallacy of this. The analogy between a small, dark cell and the womb seems to have escaped the attention it deserves. But it is no interesting little fact like those so dear to Ripley. It is a mountain of facts which would take a century to untangle.

There is the criminal, standing before the so-called bar of justice. He is a human being with head and arms and legs. He is the *fait accompli*. There is no use wishing that his father had been more careful. There is no use deploring the fact that Nature gave him oxygen to breathe and food to eat.

But still, society wants no more of the fellow. Obviously there is only one thing to be done on the face of it, only one wholly sensible thing. Kill him and let the ministers wonder vaguely if he ever had a soul. However, the crime was not that great. The judge wishes to be rid of him for only a short time, supposing in some lofty and doubtlessly marvelous process of reasoning that a few years in the cell will allow the fellow to again be born as a completely different person. It is to be wondered, then, why judges seem forever angered when the same fellow, five years later, again stands before the bar of justice awaiting another "Society wishes you had never been born."

The masses, whose will the judge executes, have contrived to remain astonishingly in the dark, along with most of their psychiatrists, about a host of facts emanating from this rather indecent wish.

The individual man thinks of a cell simply as a place where the criminal will be held incommunicado until he is finally reborn. It rarely occurs to this individual man that he is actually fostering the practice of placing this one criminal in the society of criminals. That the single criminal contacts very few of his fellow felons outside the prison walls never seems to have any bearing on the situation.

It is not a new thought that the criminal meets many of his kind in prison and learns from them many things which he before but dimly suspected.

However, when that fact is arrayed with others, the light begins to flare up.

Many men in many offices under many chiefs have been busy for many years compiling crime statistics. It is doubtful if the tabulated results are meant to bring any more order into the world. The numbers and percentages are mainly intended to show the public that men are actually tabulating such things and that therefore much thought, energy and result is being obtained and hoarded in return for certain salaries to be paid out of the public treasury.

That something can be done with those figures seems obvious enough. Then, it would seem to follow, why isn't something done?

We learn, roughly, that the criminal of today, by a large majority, ranges between the ages of twenty-four and eighteen.

By applied humanity, perhaps it is possible to understand why a boy at eighteen will turn to crime. Is it possible that it is directly related to the wish of society that he has never been born?

Oh, certainly not that! It is much too obvious. These things must be couched in polysyllabic sentences by men so overburdened with degrees that they wear out ten pens a day signing their names.

"It is not a new thought that the criminal meets many of his kind in prison and learns from them many things which he before but dimly suspected."

Certainly there can be no foundation for the idle statement that all true things are the easiest.

But just suppose that there is some truth in this.

The individual man looks hazily at the rest of society. To himself he is clear and important and very much a unit. But in a haphazard way he believes that all the people around him are different than he. They are all tied together and he is the only person in the world who is wholly alone.

And because he must live in his own flesh house for more or less three score and ten, he knows he will have to associate with a tyrannical mind perilously close to the end of his nose.

Therefore he never blames himself for anything. If he sinks a hatchet into the head of his firstborn, strangles his wife, rapes the lady of his best friend and then embezzles the funds of his firm for the getaway, he utterly believes himself when he tells the world that he is being oppressed.

If she takes out her husband's new car and dents a fender, putting it back in the garage, she soars into a tantrum, throws things and feels very abused if her husband mildly cautions her to be more careful next time.

What, then, is the thought process of an eighteen-year-old boy when his elders show such astonishing lack of good sense?

He was placed, at the age of five, in a school. And there he was taught, along with his alphabet, that he would grow up to be an important citizen in this world. At home he is usually expected to amount to something when he "grows up."

He carries this innocent-appearing virus with him into his teens and, finding himself close to manhood and an important seat in the sun, he allows the germs to breed beyond all hope of inoculation against them.

And then at sixteen or seventeen or eighteen, uncouth truth rises like a concrete wall before him and he runs into it and bruises himself.

Experience, in a gagging dose, has informed him that there are only two people in the world who care whether he lives or dies. But he cannot always lean back upon his father and mother for the necessary feeling of importance.

Then comes a variety of things, never identical from case to case. A third person makes eyes at him and he wants to have money, which is denied him through the regular channels because the world does not care to give him a job. He wishes to appear important or daring among his fellows. He has a real, crying need for money and is hungry or cold.

That is the extent of his criminality at the moment. He is young and has therefore not had a long and battering experience to tell him that the easiest money is to be gained by the hardest sweat. He is not thinking of himself as a collective piece of society. He is an individual and *needs* something.

It is easy for him to credit himself with greater cunning than he actually possesses. After all, he knows nothing of LAW. He has heard of fingerprints only in a detective story.

Very well, the world has defaulted. He has been gypped. The job he was always led to believe he would get was only a mirage. Therefore everything else is a lie and society is bad in that it gives never a damn what happens to him as long as he stays out of the way.

Combined with that, he is bored. Life, he does not know, is a very drab and dreary affair as long as Man stays on the wide but crowded sidewalk.

Thus he steps out and commits his first crime.

His hand is shaking so he can't see the front sight of his rusty .22 pistol. He can only hear the roar of blood in his ears and sounds which were never sounded. He forgets where he should look for the money. He makes too much noise. He can't control his voice.

Gasping with nervous exhaustion, he runs away and, behind closed doors, stares at the few tattered bills. Still, they are his by right of possession. In getting them, he has obeyed a natural need for excitement or food or clothing or that necessary front before his girl or his friends.

And now comes the deciding factor in his life.

The police either catch him or they do not.

If he eludes them, he may try another "job" or two, emboldened by his first success. But in an astonishingly short space of time he will run up against a "tough one." In a stickup of park spooners, the man tells him to go to hell and grabs for the gun; the youngster gets away and vows to stray no more. In a filling station, the attendant reaches for a wrench and again the youth flees in terror. In a majority of these cases, the youngster thereupon lays away the .22 forevermore and a few years later looks back with a private grin and perhaps even an uneasy twinge about his "crime career."

If he is caught, he is doomed.

Standing soaked with nervous sweat, he looks up at the judge in a black robe remarkably like a vulture's rusty wings. The youth is actually hearing, "You are hereby sentenced..."

As soon as he can bring himself to believe that this is really life and not a nightmare, he begins to believe the words really were, "Society wishes you had never been born." Not in those actual words, of course. But the feeling is there.

From the time he began to think about crime until now, the thought that the world did not want him was but partly felt. The whole impact of that truth strikes him now.

Society does not want him. He was right!

In a most lofty fashion, a judge on a bench, wondering what his wife will have for dinner, has completed the metamorphosis of the youth's ideals.

He is a ripe freshman for the Crime College. No professor of hooeyology was ever confronted with such an ardent student.

In the big, sullen pile of gray rock, the youth discovers that there is a strata of society which actually wants him. He has never seen a real criminal before and the actuality awes him. He hears men talk pridefully of stickups. He receives the usual treatment meted out to all freshmen. He's small-time.

Through the courtesy of the state, in penitentiary or reform school, the youth receives a thorough working over. By the time he graduates, his lifework is definitely planned for him. He is a snow-eater or a pervert or a tough case, but most certainly ready, in most instances, to prove himself worthy of the only fraternity which ever took any interest in him.

There comes a second crisis in his life.

On his first half-dozen jobs with the friends of his friends, he must assume the most dangerous posts and missions. Therefore he stands an excellent chance of being either shot down or picked up by the vigilant, brave and intelligent police.

"*Let it suffice to say that discipline instead of criminal education via the prison has changed the destiny of many more men than are willing to admit it.*"

Should he come through this test by fire, he is a wiser man. And as war develops cunning in an "individual fighter" so that he outlasts the rest of his company under any conditions, so does experience serve as a shield for the, by now, hardened criminal.

Quite naturally he follows the only profession in which he ever had a thorough training. No matter how many times he is caught, his sense of importance forbids him to think that it will happen again. That he is caught, again and again, is inevitable, just as inevitable as the fact that a parole board will turn him loose.

He returns to jail as a graduate returns to his alma mater and there is more truth than wit in that. It is most amazing to listen to these men sit and exchange notes.

"Thirty-three? Yeah, I was in Leavenworth. Jimmy Fenton was there."

"Was he? Well, I'll be damned. Him and me were in Alcatraz. We had a tough screw there...."

And equally astonishing is the appearance of these fellows. One kindly old gentleman had an extensive-enough list of "jobs" to send him to four leading pens.

It is an unhappy failing of the Anglo-Saxon to insist upon a solution being presented with every advanced problem.

There are many more solutions than the easy, stumbling, stupid one of sending a youngster in his teens to jail. There are enough such solutions to fill an encyclopedia. But so educated or uneducated has the human race become that the return-him-to-the-womb wish predominates to such an extent that most men are unconscious of any other solution.

Let it suffice to say that discipline instead of criminal education via the prison has changed the destiny of many more men than are willing to admit it.

One youngster, at the moment serving four years in the United States Marine Corps, started his crime career stealing cars and generally annoying the police and public. A judge told him that he would either get two years in the pen or four years in the Marines and for him to take his choice. As a Marine he has an unblemished record, has risen by his intelligence to be a corporal and when last seen was studying diverse matters concerning useful endeavor in the civilian world.

The USMC will probably rise up to a man, from the dawn to the setting sun, to condemn that exposure. Not many youths have had the luck of that corporal and the cases are pitifully few where a youth had a chance to choose. The corporal had a few tough sergeants at Parris Island to take all the nonsense out of him and he emerged a healthy, straight-thinking fellow.

There is also the prison colony system, so regrettably abused by France and England. The failure of the prison colony does not lie in its principle, but in its application. A sane man will turn mad in French Guiana, even if he be "free." No human being could survive the jungles of Tasmania when natural hazards are supplemented by overlord keepers with shoot-to-kill orders and unhealthy appetites of their own.

There is one prison colony which did survive to a remarkable degree. But the word must be whispered, as it is today, though first settled by "criminals," the most crime-free continent in the world—which would seem to dispose of the heredity theory.

There are more roads to be built, more dams to be raised in these United States than a hundred million men could finish in a thousand years. This implies criminal labor. But is criminal labor to be judged and discarded without a second thought when the conditions under which it is practiced rival French Guiana?

Can a man keep his self-respect when he is chained by the ankle to his fellow? When a guard stands near with a gun? When no thoughtfulness is shown to him? And last and most important, when his work is Labor, not Accomplishment?

There is Alaska, a land of great opportunities but seemingly in great need of a population and willing workers.

Ah, no, I venture upon dangerous ground.

Of *course* the only system is to wish that the malefactor had never been born. The mere fact that he *is* born and has grown to man's estate has no bearing upon it whatever.

Naturally we actually care very little about who forms the rank and file of organized crime. We don't give a snap of the fingers if our house is robbed or our child kidnapped. Why shouldn't we board and room and pay the tuition of youngsters in the College of Crime?

One small fact, if proved, will have no possible bearing upon the situation: If the number of criminals within our borders has decreased since the formation of the C.C.C., duly allowing for the natural increase in all ranks of crime bred by the humility of relief and the increased need and suffering of families everywhere.

No, that would have nothing to do with it whatever.

We, the people, plead, beg, demand that the practice of wishing stumbling youth had never been born retain its honorable position upon the unquestionably accurate law books of these great and glorious United States, the land where all men are created equal. ✍

"Naturally we actually care very little about who forms the rank and file of organized crime. We don't give a snap of the fingers if our house is robbed or our child kidnapped. Why shouldn't we board and room and pay the tuition of youngsters in the College of Crime?"

CHAPTER TWO

Ethics and
JUSTICE

Ethics and
Justice

I**N CONSIDERING CRIMINALITY,** LRH **TELLS US WE ARE** ultimately considering the larger questions of right and wrong, good and evil. And when we, in turn, consider such questions, we are touching upon the basis of all philosophy: ethics, justice and our optimum survival along every avenue of existence. With that in mind,

it is only appropriate that we now further consider what Ron himself brought to this matter of ethics and justice, and what he very literally maintained as the only means to guarantee "the future of this culture as a whole."

Although both ethics and justice are generally treated in several earlier papers (and fairly extensively throughout "Excalibur"), his first practical discussion of the matter came in 1944. The circumstances, as one might imagine, were war related and the setting was Princeton University, where Ron had been attending the United States Naval School of Military Government in preparation for

command in occupied territories. Although eventual combat wounds would finally preclude him from serving with American occupation forces, how those forces were to best conduct themselves with respect to ethics and justice was very carefully considered.

Broadly, he addressed the subject along two avenues: first, the employment of military justice on an occupied people irrespective of local traditions. And second, the indigenous tradition into which occupational justice must be leveled. To properly consider the latter, however, it is necessary to briefly backtrack and consider

Left
Princeton University, where, in 1944, then Lieutenant L. Ron Hubbard attended the United States Naval School of Military Government

Ron's experience as a youth in those Asian lands his nation was about to occupy.

As noted, and as part of the greater trail of discovery to Dianetics and Scientology, Ron actually spent the better part of his teenage years in Asia—particularly China and the various South Pacific islands eventually wrested from Japanese control. Through the course of these travels, he was able to observe both Japanese and Chinese judicial procedures and thus able to write from Princeton: "In my own experience, I have never heard of anything equal to the power and cruelty of Chinese justice unless it were that of Gómez [tyrannical dictator Gen. Juan Vicente Gómez] in Venezuela. The individual's apparent lack of rights before the bar of justice in Chefoo, Peking, Nagasaki or other Oriental cities has never failed to astonish me." Not mentioned, but worth noting here for emphasis, is the fact he had personally witnessed a Chinese execution; apparently it had taken place in the streets of Shanghai and would seem to have been a fairly impromptu beheading of a political offender.

Nevertheless, he points out with some vehemence, Asian conceptions of justice, and particularly the Chinese, are not devoid of liberalism.* In fact, and specifically drawn from the *Tao,* the Chinese could boast a profoundly enlightened tradition wherein each citizen was said to possess his own innate sense of right and wrong. Hence Ron's admonishment to future Western military governors: For all the infamy of Oriental justice, with its emphasis on terrible physical punishment, no US military commission or provost court should imagine Western judicial methods and standards to be "special items, grandly conceived by Western pens and functioning only in our hemisphere." Rather, "Persistently, constantly, for nearly three thousand years their identities and similarities have occurred in the thought of the Orient."

He went on to suggest much more, including a typical LRH appeal for general tolerance and the preservation of individual liberty. Yet given, as we have said, he was not to serve with those occupational forces and given, too, the intensification of Dianetics research, it was not actually until 1951 that he once more specifically addressed himself to the theory of ethics.

---

*Chinese "Liberalism" and Chinese "Conservatism" might better have been called "Taoism" and "Ju Chia" respectively, as they are intended to specify in this sense what we would call Western "Democracy" and Western "Fascism." —L. Ron Hubbard

His vehicle was *Science of Survival.* Oriented around his Chart of Human Evaluation that describes the various human emotional tones, the work offered the first accurate means of predicting human behavior. It also offered detailed explanation of the various dynamics of human existence—which is to say, the various fields or entities one must cooperate with for optimum survival. Thus we find survival is accomplished along several routes, including survival as self, as family, as a group, as Mankind and as part of all living things. And from that view of life as interdependent upon all else came the first workable definition of ethics: "Rationality toward the highest level of survival for the individual, the future race, the group and Mankind and the other dynamics taken collectively."

Lest the point be missed, however, the key concept here was *workability*. As Ron has very correctly pointed out, ethics has traditionally been a contemplative matter with more or less endless debate on what precisely constitutes right and wrong. Then, too, the subject has been hopelessly confused with justice, which is yet another matter entirely, i.e., justice is the action taken on an individual by the group when that individual fails to conduct himself in an ethical manner. Thus ethics becomes a personal matter and consists of those actions one takes upon himself for optimum survival across the whole of his dynamics. By extension, then, *good* may

Above
L. Ron Hubbard's *Science of Survival:* oriented around the Hubbard Chart of Human Evaluation. Here was the first accurate means of predicting human behavior.

be defined as constructive survival action, while evil is precisely the opposite. In other words, and this again from LRH, "Things are good which

Then again, as Ron reminds us, because Man is basically good, "when he finds himself committing too many evils, then, causatively,

"Things are good which complement the survival of the individual, his family, children, group, Mankind, life and matter, energy, space and time [the physical universe]."

complement the survival of the individual, his family, children, group, Mankind, life and matter, energy, space and time [the physical universe]." While evil is "anything which is destructive more than it is constructive along any of the various dynamics."

The net result is ethics, not as a subject for contemplation—a matter of relative abstracts, as the psychologist would say—but a functional tool for real life. What is the argument for honesty and decency? Why is theft always, ultimately, unprofitable and murder even less so? Why is the despoiling of an environment so reprehensible, not to mention the ruination of a planet? Because when one carries the ethical equation out to the last critical digit, our optimum survival as individuals is absolutely interdependent upon all else, and only by constantly considering the survival of the many can we ensure our own survival.

unconsciously or unwittingly, Man puts ethics in on himself by destroying himself." By way of example, he points to the criminal who habitually leaves clues for his own undoing or the tyrannical dictator who drives himself mad. But factually, he adds, the phenomena is universal and the cases innumerable. Having harmed too many, too often, and failing any real means to right their wrongs, men will directly and deliberately bring themselves to ruin.

It was from this vantage point, then, this grand view of ethics as reason itself, that we come to the crowning LRH achievement: the actual Ethics Technology by which survival can be bettered. An historical precedent—but bearing in mind that what Ron now brought to the subject is wholly new—he refers us to the ancient Buddhist text, *Vinaya Pitaka,* and, in particular, *Cullavagga,* or the rules of conduct for the purity of monastic life under Buddha.

According to tradition, it was the Buddha himself who authored the *Cullavagga* when the ethical lapse of disciples had been brought to his notice. Included are provisions for all major offenses as well as the more common breaches of monastic etiquette. But what distinguishes the document, and why it is relevant here, is that it constitutes one of the first (and very rare) attempts to develop an ethical system, not for punishment, but for *rehabilitation.* Thus, in addition to delineating the infringements, the *Vinaya Pitaka* also prescribes the method of atonement.

In one sense, the LRH Ethics Technology provides the same: To those who have been ostracized from a group owing to unethical conduct, Ron very definitely provides the route back home. But he also provides much, much more. In fact, with the LRH Ethics Technology comes not a means for ethical salvation through atonement, but true rehabilitation through an understanding and application of what amounts to the fundamental laws of this universe.

To explain: In very simple terms, when one speaks of survival, one is not speaking of a static state. Rather, these are definite degrees of ethical conduct and thus levels of survival. Consequently, one may be surviving more or less well but can still enjoy much improvement. With LRH ethics, then, comes not only the delineation of these various ethical states or *conditions,* but the exact steps or formulas one takes to better a condition.

In all, he has named twelve such conditions: from a state of utter Confusion wherein one is incapable of constructive action, through Treason ensuing from betrayal after trust, and thereon through successive higher conditions of Enemy, Doubt, Liability, Non-Existence, Danger, Emergency, Normal and Affluence—until finally reaching a state of unshakable Power. The point, and it is absolutely demonstrable: however low one ethically descends, one can rehabilitate through conscientious application of L. Ron Hubbard's Condition Formulas. Moreover, the formulas are applicable to anyone and any endeavor, for they reflect natural and inextricable laws governing the survival of all things—how they grow or diminish, prosper or perish. Thus although originally codified for use within Scientology organizations, employment of these conditions truly knows no bounds. In point of fact, even seemingly incorrigible criminals have rehabilitated themselves to states wherein their productivity, ethical presence and self-respect is all but palpable.

Naturally complementing LRH Ethics Technology is L. Ron Hubbard's system of justice. As he explains it: "When the individual fails to put in his own ethics, the group takes action against him and this is called justice." As the statement implies, justice is only used until such time as one's own ethics "render him fit company for his fellows." Otherwise, and herein lay what he decried as the failure of justice from Hammurabi forward, "Justice becomes an end-all in itself." The comment is crucial and cuts right to the heart of all we find objectionable in modern justice systems, including: justice as an instrument for popular revenge and/or a somewhat clogged drain into which to dispose of undesirables. In either

case, as LRH so pointedly adds: "There is little thought of administering justice so that individuals can improve."

The statistics, of course, bear him out: notwithstanding popular conceptions that stiff penalties equal reform, in fact the opposite is true. To wit: the longer the sentence, the greater tendency towards recidivism. But either way, and as noted, at least half of those discharged from American prisons will find themselves rearrested within three years of release; while special-category rates run substantially higher, e.g., some 80 percent of those with multiple arrests will find their rap sheets growing ever longer. All of which, in turn, is to say that notwithstanding billions spent on penal correction, that phrase *correctional facility* is the worst sort of oxymoron.

The LRH solution is a system of justice as equitable and workable as his system for personal ethics. Once again, although originally designed for use within Scientology organizations, the principles are applicable to any circumstance. Included are the proper gradients of justice actions according to degree of severity, the theory and practice of petition as a means of seeking redress from wrongs and the delineation of awards and penalties according to production. Also, of course, included are the tools for rehabilitation through justice to a point of personal ethics whereupon, as LRH reiterates, "justice no longer becomes the all-important subject that it is made out to be."

All notions of ethics and justice, Ron once remarked, have traditionally had but one of two aims: to cut off a head or bestow a pardon. In this peculiar age of "enlightened barbarism," as he so aptly puts it, the machinations may have grown exceptionally complex, what with rituals of plea bargaining and appeal. But when it all comes down to brass tacks—to that grimly resounding gavel on the bench—the ends are only twofold: punishment or reprieve. It comes as no small statement, then, to say: here is the means by which "Man *can* learn how to put his own ethics in and climb back up the chute." Here is the "brand-new result, the like of which nobody ever dreamed of."

The fundamental technology by which those results are obtained may be found in L. Ron Hubbard's *Introduction to Scientology Ethics*. Extending from that body of technology and resting upon the very same principles is L. Ron Hubbard's program for criminal reform. As noted, it is predicated on his lynchpin discovery that no man is inherently evil and none lack an innate sense of ethics. Consequently and very simply: "The individual can learn this technology, learn to apply it to his life and can then put his own ethics in, change conditions and start heading upwards toward survival under his own steam." ∎

In dramatic emphasis of what L. Ron Hubbard presents in his 1969 "Riots" were the 1992 Los Angeles riots sparked by the acquittal of law enforcement officers accused of beating black motorist Rodney King. Indeed, when copies of the article were broadly distributed among stricken LA residents, more than a few assumed it had been written after the 1992 burning and looting. In that regard, and yet again, LRH was not merely commenting on disturbing events, he was revealing root causes.

RIOTS

by L. RON HUBBARD

RIOTS ARE NOT ALWAYS caused by economic deprivation.

The bulk of American riots are caused by injustice.

Only the wealthy can afford justice. It may say there must be justice in the Constitution, but it can only be obtained in upper courts.

The little fellow doesn't have $100,000 to fight the unjust actions of those in power.

Until there is justice for the little people, not just for the rich, there will be riots. And these riots can easily swell into complete raw, red revolution.

A black person can be innocently standing on a street corner. Can be grabbed, beaten, thrown in jail and worked at hard labor all on some imaginary charge. It may say it can't be done in the law books, but where's his $100,000 to take it high enough for action?

I have seen a Filipino university professor hauled in for nothing, his jaw broken, held without bail, all because he was a Filipino in a white US community (Port Orchard, Washington).

I have seen jails full of men who could not even say what the actual charge against them was—but they worked like dogs every day as convict labor.

As a minister, going amongst the people, I have witnessed enough injustice to overturn a state, only waiting for a spark to ignite the suppressed wrath into revolution.

Until justice applies to all, until a person is really assumed innocent until proven guilty, until it no longer costs a tenth of a million to get to an upper court, the government is at risk.

> *"I have seen jails full of men who could not even say what the actual charge against them was—but they worked like dogs every day as convict labor."*

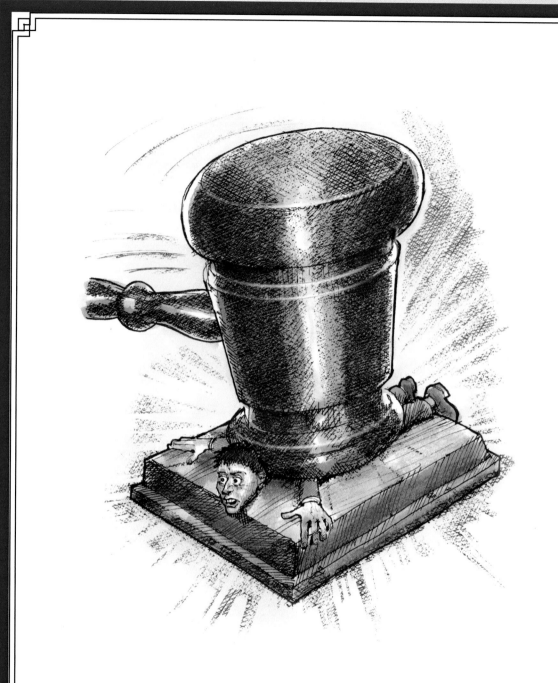

"Only the wealthy can afford justice. It may say there must be justice in the Constitution, but it can only be obtained in upper courts. The little fellow doesn't have $100,000 to fight the unjust actions of those in power."

They may be very big, their sweat may have no odor, their arrogance may put them above all others, but the leaders of a nation who, for one instant, tolerate injustice to their poorest citizens today should have their heads ready for the basket. Another 1789 is boiling up, only waiting for one big spark to flash across the Western world.

Injustice is not something in which any man with power should ever trade. It is not just a sin. It is suicide.

"I have for a very long time studied the causes of violence and conflict amongst individuals and nations," wrote L. Ron Hubbard in the winter of 1968. Accordingly, and directly drawn from that research, comes "Justice." Originally published in the Church of Scientology's Freedom magazine, the essay has particular relevance to an era when fears of terrorism have so fully eclipsed the Communist menace that false accusations are yet again the order of the day. Then, too, and notwithstanding more than half a century of progress in the name of civil rights, we are still discussing an American criminal-justice system that is more than five times as likely to find black males guilty of crimes as their white counterparts.

JUSTICE

by L. RON HUBBARD

THE MAJOR BREAKDOWN OF Western democracy is its habit of carelessly basing legal actions on false reports.

Anyone can say anything about anybody, and police powers and courts are liable to act on reports so false that a child could see through the lie.

This was the most odious thing about the **NAZIS**. And this characterizes Communist "justice."

In February 1969, I isolated the false accusation, false report and failing to confront the accused with his accusers as the basic breakdown of justice. These undermine personal security and involve the whole judiciary in endless, needless traffic.

Innocent people are subjected to press attacks, court procedures, endless expense and ruined lives by these factors alone.

Corrupt pressure groups, such as the psychiatrists, can disrupt any possible rival or tear the social structure of a nation to pieces as long as false reports are published, accepted and acted upon.

So flagrant is this abuse that it destroys, for one and all, the value of the cause of democracy.

When justice becomes slow, when it becomes expensive and when false reports on people and groups are allowed to go unchallenged and unpunished, any ideology becomes a tyranny.

So great are these factors in the disruption of loyalty and creation of revolutionaries that no government that permits them is safe.

This is, in fact, a new philosophic breakthrough in the field of jurisprudence. The great importance of the false report in breaking down a nation's social structure and its cause has not been understood.

Most of the internal conflict in a country is caused by individuals and groups defending themselves against false reports.

In a period where governments "seek to capture the minds of men," a great deal of reform will have to be done.

Human rights have as one of their threats the false report. Yet there is no adequate practical recourse. Suits for libel? Forget them. They cost more than anyone can afford, take forever to try and leave the public with the false reports even when they are won.

As false reports tear down the security of the individual and small group, these then have to assert themselves. They do so, in their turn, by attacking.

"When justice becomes slow, when it becomes expensive and when false reports on people and groups are allowed to go unchallenged and unpunished, any ideology becomes a tyranny."

A nation which permits these to be acted upon will eventually find itself deserted by its populace and supporting groups, attacked by its decent people and eventually will be overthrown.

To save itself, a nation must permit direct legal action which is fast and inexpensive so that an individual or group can legally protect itself from false reports.

Only if the "free" world reforms its human rights will it have a cause worth fighting for, worth supporting. Otherwise its public and social groups will desert it to any other cause without even much examining it.

The virtues of patriotism, loyalty and devotion to the government are not dead by some strange social decay. They are dead because people feel their government no longer protects them, even attacks them, opens the door on them to easy psychiatric seizure, fantastic taxation and personal insecurity.

For instance, the black man in the US has long been saying he will not fight for the government. That isn't because he's a Communist. It's because anyone can lay a charge on them, no matter how false, get a black man jailed, beaten up, lynched. And authorities shrugged with "It's just a coon." He had no equal *respect* under law. Any false report, untested, could get him arrested, beaten or killed. So he became very insecure. And now he continually riots, loots, burns, is even closing universities. All because any false report was accepted. And he could be beaten or hung waiting on slow, expensive justice.

It isn't limited to US blacks. This was true of all US minority groups and is true of religious and racial minority groups in far too many countries. So they form a core of resistance and unrest. They are nervous and defensive.

Then, as the situation worsens, many social groups begin to react to false reports against them, again unable to obtain justice fast enough to prevent name damage.

About that time the officials better look to their foreign bank accounts and decamp. For that government, even while still functioning, is no longer the government of its people. It is their enemy. Any revolutionary movement will be joined. These are the mechanics of revolution.

People will stand for an awful lot. Then one day patriotism is dead. Because the government no longer has a cause the majority believe in or will fight for.

The principles of not accepting false reports and confronting one with his accusers and their accusations *before* punishing actions of any kind are so strong that if the West accepted them and scrupulously practiced them, IT WOULD HAVE A CAUSE GREAT ENOUGH TO SURVIVE.

It could then "out-cause" the Communist.

As it stands, Western governments have to BUY and BRIBE their defense at a cost so fantastic it will break them.

Our position is this: We are standing up and befriending Western powers, trying to get them to pull up their honor and justice before the mob gets to them and tears them to bits.

From what amounted to some fifty years of research into questions of ethics, justice and the ideal social contract, LRH authored this immensely meaningful document for the establishment of a model Penal Code. Previously, he had authored ideal constitutions for three emerging African nations and lectured extensively on matters relating to liberty and the preservation of political freedom. Those familiar with the lectures, or the larger body of his work on ethics, will recognize the salient points: punishment solves nothing, vindictive justice is no justice at all and no state has a moral right to take a human life.

PENAL CODE

by L. Ron Hubbard

THIS PENAL CODE OF the Constitution is based on the principle that all men are equal under law, regardless of privilege, wealth, descent, antecedents, repute or poverty and that no costs, conditions, rumor or publicity shall swerve favorably or unfavorably the course of justice or the rights thereto.

Each person, citizen or alien, regardless of age, color, creed or repute, shall have:

1. A fair hearing for any misdemeanor requiring fine or discipline before an unbiased magistrate.

2. A fair trial, adequately defended, before an unbiased judge and jury, for any felony or capital crime.

3. The right of habeas corpus without delay, regardless of the charge, reason or method of his or her seizure.

4. Sanity and insanity alike, regardless of how pronounced, shall have no bearing whatever in the issue of warrants, seizure, detention, defense, exculpation or sentence and, in itself, insanity may be no charge for any warrant, seizure or confinement. The acts of a person shall be judged entirely and alone as acts within the meaning of misdemeanor, felony or capital crime, tried and sentenced without any attention or heed to any difference such as capability, sanity, youth or age. The mental attitude or condition, however asserted, shall have no bearing upon or place in law.

5. No public official, agent elected, hired or appointed, part, department or division of a government, including the government itself, may act in any manner to exceed, set aside or ignore any part of this Constitution and in such case of violation, individually or collectively, the matter shall become one of criminal or civil procedure as the consequences of the act are found to merit before any low or high court, and no summons may be refused by any

court to prevent justice from occurring, such departures by officials or the government being themselves the nullification of all rights of the citizen with consequent tyranny.

6. Parliamentary and/or Congressional efforts to thwart, deny or nullify the Constitution or its Penal Code, purposes or rights subject the individual members thereof to discipline within this code and the acts to nullification.

7. It shall be a felony to subvert, ignore or alter this Constitution.

8. Theft or damage or loss by omission or commission of persons' property interests or funds, but not exceeding the value of a month's salary by an average citizen, shall be deemed a misdemeanor and is punishable by a fine payable to the damaged parties and all fees and costs of the action.

9. Theft or malicious damage or loss by omission or commission beyond that of a month's salary of an average citizen shall be punishable as a felony and if proven beyond reasonable doubt, shall result in a restriction order on the person until the damage is paid in full with all costs and fees.

10. Personal physical injury of a person by passion or malice shall be judged a crime and, if incapacitating, shall result in a fine of double the usual pay of the victim for the time he or she is incapacitated whether the pay continues elsewhere or not or in such compensatory award as the judge may allocate.

11. Loss of life through negligence or without intention shall be deemed a felony or as the judge may declare commensurate with extenuation.

12. Loss of life by intent shall be deemed a capital crime and shall be actionable by a total reimbursement of loss of their interest to all financially involved persons and substitution insofar as possible by the offender and, failing the latter, shall be further disciplined as the judge of the court, after due unanimous findings by the jury, shall decree.

13. The death sentence shall not be part of any Penal Code of the country.

14. Treason shall be defined as any knowing effort to overthrow the Constitution, as subversion of the state in the interest of a foreign power or willful and malicious betrayal of the national interest to the benefit of forces seeking to overthrow the Constitution or secret employment or retention by a foreign enemy or betraying the nation or an employer for pay or revenge. It shall be deemed a capital crime and, proven beyond reasonable doubt before a jury, shall be punishable by deprivation of all property, of any citizenship and exile or as the judge may decree.

15. Seeking, by libel and slander or false public utterances, to deprive a person of his constitutional rights or his livelihood or his public esteem shall be deemed a felony.

16. Depriving, by libel, slander, false statements or any persuasion, a person of his or her legal spouse or family members or family shall be deemed a felony.

> *"This Penal Code of the Constitution is based on the principle that all men are equal under law, regardless of privilege, wealth, descent, antecedents, repute or poverty and that no costs, conditions, rumor or publicity shall swerve favorably or unfavorably the course of justice or the rights thereto."*

17. The forceful removal of a person from his abode or the forceful detention of a person separate from his family or friends by private persons or groups acting outside the legal structure shall be deemed a felony; and kidnapping for ransom or favors shall be deemed a capital offense.

18. Forceful physical treatment not resulting in a well and restored being shall be deemed a felony.

19. Physical treatment which damages or injures a personality shall be deemed a felony.

20. Advising or coaxing or introducing the use of psychotropic or hallucinatory drugs, weeds or chemical preparations shall be deemed a felony and the purveyance of such shall be deemed a capital crime.

21. Educating youth against the national interest and Constitution shall be deemed a felony.

22. No person may be detained or incarcerated on the possibility of his committing a crime which in fact has not been committed.

23. The committing of genocide shall be deemed a capital crime.

Presuming, as put forth in Scientology, that Man is essentially an immortal spirit with experience well beyond a single lifetime, we all possess an infinite ability to survive. Yet how well we survive, L. Ron Hubbard explains, is dependent upon ethics. In summary of this truly monumental view of ethics as the means by which we may flourish forever comes his "Ethics, Justice and the Dynamics."

ETHICS, JUSTICE AND THE DYNAMICS

by L. RON HUBBARD

Survival

The Dynamic Principle of Existence is: SURVIVE!

No behavior or activity has been found to exist without this principle. It is not new that life is surviving. It is new that life has as its entire dynamic urge *only* survival.

It is as though, at some remarkably distant time, the Supreme Being gave forth a command to all life: "Survive!" It was not said how to survive nor yet how long. All that was said was "Survive!" The reverse of "Survive!" is "Succumb." And that is the penalty for not engaging in survival activities.

An individual survives or succumbs in ratio to his ability to acquire and hold the wherewithal of survival. The security of a good job, for instance, means some guarantee of survival—other threats to existence not becoming too overpowering. The man who makes a good living can afford better clothing against the weather, a sounder and better home, medical care for himself and his family, good transportation and, what is important, the respect of his fellows. All these things are survival.

The Eight Dynamics

As one looks out across the confusion which is life or existence to most people, one can discover eight main divisions.

There could be said to be eight urges (drives, impulses) in life.

These we call *dynamics*.

These are motives or motivations.

We call them *the eight dynamics.*

There is no thought or statement here that any one of these eight dynamics is more important than the others. While they are categories (divisions) of the broad game of life, they are not necessarily equal to each other. It will be found amongst individuals that each person stresses one of the dynamics more than the others, or may stress a combination of dynamics as more important than other combinations.

The purpose in setting forth this division is to increase an understanding of life by placing it in compartments. Having subdivided existence in this fashion, each compartment can be inspected (as itself and by itself) in its relationship to the other compartments of life.

In working a puzzle, it is necessary to first take pieces of similar color or character and place them in groups. In studying a subject, it is necessary to proceed in an orderly fashion.

To promote this orderliness, it is necessary to assume (for our purposes) these eight arbitrary compartments of life.

The First Dynamic is the urge toward existence as one's self. Here we have individuality expressed fully. This can be called the *Self Dynamic.*

The Second Dynamic is the urge toward existence as a sexual activity. This dynamic actually has two divisions. Second Dynamic (a) is the sexual act itself. And the Second Dynamic (b) is the family unit, including the rearing of children. This can be called the *Sex Dynamic.*

The Third Dynamic is the urge toward existence in groups of individuals. Any group, or part of an entire class, could be considered to be a part of the Third Dynamic. The school, the society, the town, the nation are each *part* of the Third Dynamic and each one *is* a Third Dynamic. This can be called the *Group Dynamic.*

The Fourth Dynamic is the urge toward existence as or of Mankind. Whereas one race would be considered a Third Dynamic, all the races would be considered the Fourth Dynamic. This can be called the *Mankind Dynamic.*

The Fifth Dynamic is the urge toward existence of the animal kingdom. This includes all living things, whether vegetable or animal, the fish in the sea, the beasts of the field or of the forest, grass, trees, flowers or anything directly and intimately motivated by *life.* This can be called the *Animal Dynamic.*

The Sixth Dynamic is the urge toward existence as the physical universe. The physical universe is composed of Matter, Energy, Space and Time. In Scientology we take the first letter of each of these words and coin a word—MEST. This can be called the *Universe Dynamic.*

The Seventh Dynamic is the urge toward existence as or of spirits. Anything spiritual, with or without identity, would come under the heading of the Seventh Dynamic. This can be called the *Spiritual Dynamic.*

The Eighth Dynamic is the urge toward existence as infinity. This is also identified as the Supreme Being. This is called the Eighth Dynamic because the symbol of infinity, ∞, stood upright makes the numeral 8. This can be called the *Infinity* or *God Dynamic.*

Scientologists usually call these by number.

A further manifestation of these dynamics is that they could best be represented as a series of concentric circles, wherein the First Dynamic would be the center and each new dynamic would be successively a circle outside it.

The basic characteristic of the individual includes his ability to so expand into the other dynamics. But when the Seventh Dynamic is reached in its entirety, one will only then discover the true Eighth Dynamic.

As an example of use of these dynamics, one discovers that a baby at birth is not perceptive beyond the First Dynamic. But as the child grows and interests extend, the child can be seen to embrace other dynamics.

As a further example of use, a person who is incapable of operating on the Third Dynamic is incapable at once of being a part of a team and so might be said to be incapable of a social existence.

As a further comment upon the eight dynamics, no one of these dynamics from one to seven is more important than any other one of them in terms of orienting the individual.

The abilities and shortcomings of individuals can be understood by viewing their participation in the various dynamics.

Gradient Scale of Right and Wrong

The word *gradient* is meant to define "lessening or increasing degrees of condition." The difference between one point on a gradient scale and another point could be as different or as wide as the entire range of the scale itself. Or it could be as tiny as to need the most minute discernment for its establishment.

Terms like *good* and *bad, alive* and *dead, right* and *wrong* are used only in conjunction with gradient scales.

On the scale of right and wrong, everything above zero or center would be more and more right, approaching an infinite rightness; and everything below zero or center would be more and more wrong, approaching an infinite wrongness. The gradient scale is a way of thinking about the universe which approximates the actual conditions of the universe more closely than any other existing logical method.

The resolution of all problems is a study in rightness and wrongness. The entire problem of getting right answers and wrong answers is a problem of degrees of rightness and wrongness.

Acts or solutions are either more right than wrong (in which case they are right) or more wrong than right (in which case they are wrong).

An ultimate wrongness for the organism would be death, not only for the organism itself, but for all involved in its dynamics. An ultimate rightness for the organism would be survival to a reasonable term for himself, his children, his group and Mankind. An **ABSOLUTE WRONGNESS** would be the extinction of the Universe and all energy and the source of energy—the infinity of complete death. An **ABSOLUTE RIGHTNESS** would be the immortality of the individual himself, his children, his group, Mankind and the Universe and all energy—the infinity of complete survival.

Graph of Logic

(Simplified for illustration)

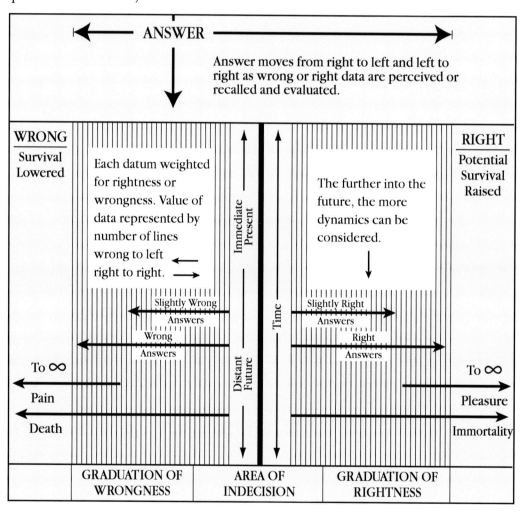

If a man, a group, a race or Mankind does its thinking on a sufficiently rational plane, it survives. And survival, that dynamic thrust through time toward some unannounced goal, is pleasure. Creative and constructive effort is pleasure.

If a man, a group or a race or Mankind does its thinking on a sufficiently irrational plane—out of lack of data, warped viewpoint or simply aberration—the survival is lessened; more is destroyed than is created. That is pain. That is the route toward death. That is evil.

Logic is not good or bad in itself, it is the name of a computation procedure: the procedure of the mind in its effort to attain solutions to problems.

Ethics, Justice and the Dynamics

Every being has an infinite ability to survive. How well he accomplishes this is dependent on how well he uses ethics on his dynamics.

Ethics Tech exists for the individual.

It exists to give the individual a way to increase his survival and thus free himself from the dwindling spiral of the current culture.

Ethics

The whole subject of ethics is one which, with the society in its current state, has become almost lost.

Ethics actually consists of rationality toward the highest level of survival for the individual, the future race, the group, Mankind and the other dynamics taken up collectively.

Ethics are reason.

Man's greatest weapon is his reason.

The highest ethic level would be long-term survival concepts with minimal destruction, along all of the dynamics.

An optimum solution to any problem would be that solution which brought the greatest benefits to the greatest number of dynamics. The poorest solution would be that solution which brought the greatest harm to the most number of dynamics.

Activities which brought minimal survival to a lesser number of dynamics and damaged the survival of a greater number of dynamics could not be considered rational activities.

One of the reasons that this society is dying and so forth, is that it's gone too far out-ethics. Reasonable conduct and optimum solutions have ceased to be used to such an extent that the society is on the way out.

By *out-ethics* we mean an action or situation in which an individual is involved, or something the individual does, which is contrary to the ideals, best interests and survival of his dynamics.

For a man to develop a weapon capable of destroying all life on this planet (as has been done with atomic weapons and certain drugs designed by the US Army) and place it in the hands of the criminally insane politicians is obviously not a survival act.

For the government to actively invite and create inflation to a point where a depression is a real threat to the individuals of this society is a non-survival action to say the least.

This gets so batty that in one of the South Pacific societies, infanticide became a ruling passion. There was a limited supply of food and they wanted to keep down the birthrate. They began using abortion and if this didn't work, they killed the children. Their Second Dynamic folded up. That society has almost disappeared.

These are acts calculated to be destructive and harmful to the survival of the people of the society.

Ethics are the actions an individual takes on himself in order to accomplish optimum survival for himself and others on all dynamics. Ethical actions are survival actions. Without a use of ethics we will not survive.

"Man is basically good. He is basically well intentioned. He does not want to harm himself or others."

We know that the Dynamic Principle of Existence is SURVIVE!

At first glance that may seem too basic. It may seem too simple. When one thinks of survival, one is apt to make the error of thinking in terms of "barest necessity." That is not survival. Survival is a graduated scale, with infinity or immortality at the top and death and pain at the bottom.

Good and Evil, Right and Wrong

Years ago I discovered and proved that Man is basically good. This means that the basic personality and the basic intentions of the individual, toward himself and others, are good.

When a person finds himself committing too many harmful acts against the dynamics, he becomes his own executioner. This gives us the proof that Man is basically good. When he finds himself committing too many evils, then, causatively, unconsciously or unwittingly, Man puts ethics in on himself by destroying himself and he does himself in without assistance from anybody else.

This is why the criminal leaves clues on the scene, why people develop strange incapacitating illnesses and why they cause themselves accidents and even decide to have an accident. When they violate their own ethics, they begin to decay. They do this all on their own, without anybody else doing anything.

The criminal who leaves clues behind is doing so in hopes that someone will come along to stop him from continuing to harm others. He is *basically* good and does not want to harm others. And in the absence of an ability to stop himself outright, he attempts to put ethics in on himself by getting thrown in prison where he will no longer be able to commit crimes.

Similarly, the person who incapacitates himself with illness or gets himself in an accident is putting ethics in on himself by lessening his ability to harm and maybe even by totally removing himself from the environment that he has been harming. When he has evil intentions, when he is being "intentionally evil," he still has an urge to also stop himself. He seeks to suppress them and when he cannot do so directly, he does so indirectly. Evil, illness and decay often go hand in hand.

Man is basically good. He is basically well intentioned. He does not want to harm himself or others. When an individual does harm the dynamics, he will destroy himself in an effort to save those dynamics. This can be proven and has been proven in innumerable cases. It is this fact which evidences that Man is basically good.

"The highest ethic level would be long-term survival concepts with minimal destruction, along all of the dynamics."

On this basis we have the concepts of right and wrong.

When we speak of ethics, we are talking about right and wrong conduct. We are talking about good and evil.

Good can be considered to be any constructive survival action. It happens that no construction can take place without some small destruction, just as the tenement must be torn down to make room for the new apartment building.

To be good, something must contribute to the individual, to his family, his children, his group, Mankind or life. To be good, a thing must contain construction which outweighs the destruction it contains. A new cure which saves a hundred lives and kills one is an acceptable cure.

Good is survival. Good is being more right than one is wrong. Good is being more successful than one is unsuccessful, along constructive lines.

Things are good which complement the survival of the individual, his family, children, group, Mankind, life and MEST.

Acts are good which are more beneficial than destructive along these dynamics.

Evil is the opposite of good, and is anything which is destructive more than it is constructive along any of the various dynamics. A thing which does more destruction than construction is evil from the viewpoint of the individual, the future race, group, species, life or MEST that it destroys.

When an act is more destructive than constructive, it is evil. It is out-ethics. When an act assists succumbing more than it assists survival, it is an evil act in the proportion that it destroys.

Good, bluntly, is survival. Ethical conduct is survival. Evil conduct is non-survival. Construction is good when it promotes survival. Construction is evil when it inhibits survival. Destruction is good when it enhances survival.

An act or conclusion is as right as it promotes the survival of the individual, future race, group, Mankind or life making the conclusion. To be entirely right would be to survive to infinity.

An act or conclusion is wrong to the degree that it is non-survival to the individual, future race, group, species or life responsible for doing the act or making the conclusion. The most wrong a person can be on the First Dynamic is dead.

The individual or group which is, on the average, more right than wrong (since these terms are not absolutes, by far) should survive. An individual who, on the average, is more wrong than right will succumb.

While there could be no absolute right or absolute wrong, a right action would depend upon its assisting the survival of the dynamics immediately concerned, a wrong action would impede the survival of the dynamics concerned.

Let us look at how these concepts of right and wrong fit into our current society.

This is a dying society. Ethics have gone so far out and are so little understood that this culture is headed for succumb at a dangerous rate.

A person is not going to come alive, this society is not going to survive, unless Ethics Tech is gotten hold of and applied.

When we look at Vietnam, inflation, the oil crisis, corruption of government, war, crime, insanity, drugs, sexual promiscuity, etc., we are looking at a culture on the way out. This is a direct result of individuals failing to apply ethics to their dynamics.

It actually starts with individual ethics.

Dishonest conduct is non-survival. Anything is unreasonable or evil which brings about the destruction of individuals, groups or inhibits the future of the race.

The keeping of one's word, when it has been sacredly pledged, is an act of survival, since one is then trusted, but only so long as he keeps his word.

To the weak, to the cowardly, to the reprehensibly irrational, dishonesty and underhanded dealings, the harming of others and the blighting of their hopes seem to be the only way of conducting life.

Unethical conduct is actually the conduct of destruction and fear. Lies are told because one is afraid of the consequences should one tell the truth. Destructive acts are usually done out of fear. Thus, the liar is inevitably a coward and the coward inevitably a liar.

"Destructive acts are usually done out of fear. Thus, the liar is inevitably a coward and the coward inevitably a liar."

The sexually promiscuous woman, the man who breaks faith with his friend, the covetous pervert are all dealing in such non-survival terms that degradation and unhappiness are part and parcel of their existence.

It probably seems quite normal and perfectly all right to some, to live in a highly degraded society full of criminals, drugs, war and insanity, where we are in constant threat of the total annihilation of life on this planet.

Well, let me say that this is not normal and it is not necessary. It *is* possible for individuals to lead happy productive lives without having to worry about whether or not they are going to be robbed if they walk outside their door or whether Russia is going to declare war on the United States. It is a matter of ethics. It is simply a matter of individuals applying ethics to their lives and having their dynamics in communication and surviving.

Morals

Now we have ethics as survival. But what of such things as morals, ideals, love? Don't these things go above "mere survival"? No, they do not.

Romantic novels and television teach us that the hero always wins and that good always triumphs. But it appears that the hero doesn't always win and that good does not always triumph. On a shorter view we can see villainy triumphing all about us. The truth of the matter is that the villainy is sooner or later going to lose. One cannot go through life victimizing one's fellow beings and wind up anything but trapped—the victim himself.

However, one doesn't observe this in the common course of life. One sees the villains succeeding everywhere, evidently amassing money, cutting their brother's throat, receiving the fruits of the courts and coming to rule over men.

Without looking at the final consequence of this, which is there just as certainly as the sun rises and sets, one begins to believe that evil triumphs whereas one has been taught that only good triumphs. This can cause the person himself to have a failure and can actually cause his downfall.

"Crime might be defined as the reduction of the survival level along any one of the eight dynamics."

As for ideals, as for honesty, as for one's love of one's fellow man, one cannot find good survival for one or for many where these things are absent.

The criminal does not survive well. The average criminal spends the majority of his adult years caged like some wild beast and guarded from escape by the guns of good marksmen.

A man who is known to be honest is awarded survival—good jobs, good friends. And the man who has his ideals, no matter how thoroughly he may be persuaded to desert them, survives well only so long as he is true to those ideals.

Have you ever seen a doctor who, for the sake of personal gain, begins to secretly attend criminals or peddle dope? That doctor does not survive long after his ideals are laid aside.

Ideals, morals, ethics, all fall within this understanding of survival. One survives so long as he is true to himself, his family, his friends, the laws of the universe. When he fails in any respect, his survival is cut down.

In the modern dictionary, we find that *ethics* are defined as "morals" and *morals* are defined as "ethics." These two words are *not* interchangeable.

Morals should be defined as a code of good conduct laid down out of the experience of the race to serve as a uniform yardstick for the conduct of individuals and groups.

Morals are actually laws.

The origin of a moral code comes about when it is discovered through actual experience that some act is more non-survival than pro-survival. The prohibition of this act then enters into the customs of the people and may eventually become a law.

In the absence of extended reasoning powers, moral codes, so long as they provide better survival for their group, are a vital and necessary part of any culture.

Morals, however, become burdensome and protested against when they become outmoded. And although a revolt against morals may have as its stated target the fact that the code no longer is as applicable as it once was, revolts against moral codes generally occur because individuals of the group or the group itself has gone out-ethics to a point where it wishes to practice license against these moral codes, not because the codes themselves are unreasonable.

If a moral code were thoroughly reasonable, it could, at the same time, be considered thoroughly ethical. But only at this highest level could the two be called the same.

The ultimate in reason is the ultimate in survival.

Ethical conduct includes the adherence to the moral codes of the society in which we live.

Justice

When an individual fails to apply ethics to himself and fails to follow the morals of the group, justice enters in.

It is not realized generally that the criminal is not only anti-social but is also anti-self.

A person who is out-ethics, who has his dynamics out of communication, is a potential or active criminal, in that crimes against the pro-survival actions of others are continually perpetrated. *Crime* might be defined as the reduction of the survival level along any one of the eight dynamics.

Justice is used when the individual's own out-ethics and destructive behavior begin to impinge too heavily on others.

In a society run by criminals and controlled by incompetent police, the citizens reactively identify any justice action or symbol with oppression.

But we have a society full of people who do not apply ethics to themselves, and in the absence of true ethics one cannot live with others and life becomes miserable. Therefore we have justice, which was developed to protect the innocent and decent.

When an individual fails to apply ethics to himself and follow the moral codes, the society takes justice action against him.

Justice, although it unfortunately cannot be trusted in the hands of Man, has as its basic intention and purpose the survival and welfare of those it serves. Justice, however, would not be needed when you have individuals who are sufficiently sane and in-ethics that they do not attempt to blunt others' survival.

Justice would be used until a person's own ethics render him fit company for his fellows.

Ethics, Justice and Your Survival

In the past, the subject of ethics has not really been mentioned very much. Justice was, however. Justice systems have long been used as a substitute for ethics systems. But when you try to substitute ethics for justice, you get into trouble.

Man has not had an actual workable way of applying ethics to himself. The subjects of ethics and justice have been terribly aberrated.

We now have the tech of Ethics and Justice straightened out. This is the only road out on the subject that Man has.

People have been trying to put ethics in on themselves for eons without knowing how. Ethics evolved with the individual's attempts at continued survival.

When a person does something which is out-ethics (harms his and others' survival), he tries to right this wrong. Usually he just winds up caving himself in. (*Caved in* means mental and/or physical collapse to the extent that the individual cannot function causatively.)

They cave themselves in because, in an effort to restrain themselves and stop themselves from committing more harmful acts, they start withdrawing and withholding themselves from the area they have harmed. A person who does this becomes less and less able to influence his dynamics and thus becomes a victim of them. It is noted here that one must have done to other dynamics those things which other dynamics now seem to have the power to do to him. Therefore he is in a position to be injured and he loses control. He can become, in fact, a zero of influence and a vacuum for trouble.

This comes about because the person does not have the basic tech of Ethics. It has never been explained to him. No one ever told him how he could get out of the hole he's gotten himself into. This tech has remained utterly unknown.

So he has gone down the chute.

Ethics is one of the primary tools a person uses to dig himself out with.

Whether he knows how to or not, every person will try to dig himself out. It doesn't matter who he is or what he's done, he is going to be trying to put ethics in on himself, one way or the other.

Even with Hitler and Napoleon, there were attempts at self-restraint. It's interesting in looking at the lives of these people how thoroughly they worked at self-destruction. The self-destruction is their attempt at applying ethics to themselves. They worked at this self-destruction on several dynamics. They can't put ethics in on themselves, they can't restrain themselves from doing these harmful acts, so they punish themselves. They realize they are criminals and cave themselves in.

All beings are basically good and are attempting to survive as best they can. They are attempting to put ethics in on their dynamics.

Ethics and justice were developed and exist to aid an individual in his urge towards survival. They exist to keep the dynamics in communication. The tech of Ethics is the actual tech of survival.

An individual's dynamics will be in communication to the degree that he is applying ethics to his life. If one knows and applies Ethics Tech to his life, he can keep the dynamics in communication and continuously increase his survival.

That is why ethics exists—so that we can survive like we want to survive, by having our dynamics in communication.

Ethics are not to be confused with justice. Justice is used only after a failure of the individual to use ethics on himself. With personal ethics in across the dynamics, Third Dynamic justice disappears as a primary concern. That's where you get a world without crime.

A man who steals from his employer has his Third Dynamic out of communication with his First Dynamic. He is headed for a prison sentence, or unemployment at best, which is not what one would call optimum survival on the First and Second Dynamic (not to mention the rest of them). He probably believes he is enhancing his survival by stealing, yet if he knew the tech of Ethics he would realize he is harming himself as well as others and will only end up further down the chute.

The man who lies, the woman who cheats on her husband, the teenager who takes drugs, the politician who is involved in dishonest dealings, all are cutting their own throats. They are harming their own survival by having their dynamics out of communication and not applying ethics to their lives.

It may come as a surprise to you, but a clean heart and clean hands are the only way to achieve happiness and survival. The criminal will never make it unless he reforms; the liar will never be happy or satisfied with himself until he begins dealing in truth.

The optimum solution to any problem presented by life would be that which leads to increased survival on the majority of the dynamics.

Thus we see that a knowledge of ethics is necessary to survival.

The knowledge and application of ethics is the way out of the trap of degradation and pain.

We can, each and every one of us, achieve happiness and optimum survival for ourselves and others by using Ethics Tech.

What Happens If the Dynamics Go Out-Ethics

It is important to remember that these dynamics comprise life. They do not operate singly without interaction with the other dynamics.

Life is a group effort. None survive alone.

If one dynamic goes out-ethics, it goes out of communication with (to a greater or lesser degree) the other dynamics. In order to remain in communication, the dynamics must remain in-ethics.

Let us take the example of a woman who has totally withdrawn from the Third Dynamic. She won't have anything to do with any groups or the people of her town. She has no friends. She stays locked in her house all day thinking (with some misguided idea of independence or individuality) that she is surviving better on her First Dynamic. Actually she is quite unhappy and lonely and lives in fear of other human beings. To ease her misery and boredom, she begins to take sedatives and tranquilizers which she becomes addicted to and then starts drinking alcohol as well.

She is busy "solving" her dilemma with further destructive actions. You can see how she has driven her First, Second and Third Dynamics out of communication. She is actively destroying her survival on her dynamics. These actions are out-ethics in the extreme, and it would not be surprising if she eventually killed herself with the deadly combination of sedatives and alcohol.

Or let us take the man who is committing destructive acts on the job. These acts need not be large, they can be as simple as showing up late for work, not doing as professional a job on each product as he is capable of, damaging equipment or hiding things from his employer. He does not have to be overtly engaged in the total destruction of the company to know that he is committing harmful acts.

Now, this man finds himself sliding more and more out-ethics as time goes along. He feels he must hide more and more and he does not know how to stop this downward spiral. Very likely it never even occurred to him that he could stop it. He is lacking the tech of Ethics. He probably doesn't realize that his actions are driving his dynamics out of communication.

This may affect his other dynamics in various ways. He will probably be a bit miserable and, since he is basically good, he will feel guilt. He goes home at night and his wife says cheerily, "How was your day?" and he cringes a little and feels worse. He starts drinking to numb the misery. He is out of communication with his family. He is out of communication on his job. His performance at work worsens. He begins to neglect himself and his belongings. He no longer gets joy out of life. His happy and satisfying life slips away from him. Because he does not know and apply Ethics Tech to his life and his dynamics, the situation goes quite out of his control. He has unwittingly become the effect of his own out-ethics. Unless he gets his life straightened out by using ethics, he will undoubtedly die a miserable man.

Now I ask you, what kind of life is that? Unfortunately, it is all too common in our current times.

A person cannot go out-ethics on a dynamic without it having disastrous consequences on his other dynamics.

It is really quite tragic, the tragedy being compounded by the fact that it is so unnecessary. If Man only knew the simple tech of Ethics, he could achieve for himself the self-respect, personal satisfaction and success that he only believes himself capable of dreaming of, not attaining.

Man is seeking survival. Survival is measured in pleasure. That means, to most men, happiness, self-respect, the personal satisfaction of a job well done and success. A man may have money, he may have a lot of personal belongings, etc., but he will not be happy unless he actually has his ethics in and knows he came by these things honestly. These rich political and financial criminals are not happy. They may be envied by the common man for their wealth, but they are very unhappy people who more often than not come to grief eventually through drug or alcohol addiction, suicide or some other means of self-destruction.

Let us look at the all-too-common current occurrence of out-ethics on the Second Dynamic. This is generally thought to be perfectly acceptable behavior.

It is easy to see how Second Dynamic out-ethics affects the other dynamics.

Let us say we have a young woman who is somewhat happily married and decides to have an affair with her boss, who happens to be a good friend of her husband. This is quite obviously out-ethics, as well as against the law, although an amazing number of people would find this sort of behavior acceptable or mildly objectionable at most.

This is quite a destructive act, however. She will suffer from guilt; she will feel deceitful and unhappy because she knows she has committed a bad act against her husband. Her relationship with him will certainly suffer and since her boss is experiencing much the same thing in his home, she and her boss will begin to feel bad towards each other as they begin to target each other for their misfortune. Their dynamics end up quite messed up and out of communication. She will feel unhappy on her First Dynamic as she has abandoned her own moral code. Her Second Dynamic will be out of communication and she may even begin to find fault with and dislike her husband. The situation at work is strained as she is now out of communication with her boss and her fellow workers. Her boss has ruined his relationship and friendship with her husband. She is so embroiled in these three dynamics that they go totally out of communication with her Fourth, Fifth and Sixth Dynamics. This is all the result of ethics going out on a single dynamic.

The repercussions spread insidiously to all the dynamics.

Our survival is assured only by our knowledge and application of ethics to our dynamics in order to keep them in communication.

Through ethics we can achieve survival and happiness for ourselves and for planet Earth.

CHAPTER THREE

Crime, Punishment and PSYCHIATRY

Crime, Punishment and
Psychiatry

IF WE ARE TO UNDERSTAND THE CRIMINAL, L. RON HUBBARD tells us, then we must finally come to grips with what has so precipitated crime: namely, psychiatry and psychology.

On the one hand, the link is as obvious as any crime-drug connection (and any savvy dealer will attest to the fact that much of his merchandise

had first been brewed in psychiatric laboratories). Ultimately, however, that link runs far deeper and actually involves the entire ideological base of psychiatric and psychological theory.

The premise is simple, insidious and fairly unbroken from Darwin, Wundt and Pavlov to all modern schools of psychiatric and psychological thought: If the human being is essentially an animal descended from an upright killer ape, then surely we must still carry some biological propensity for violence. After all, it is argued, what is the most obviously compelling force for organization in all

societies? The answer, of course, is war. (While religion is generally tossed off as a superstitious effort to obtain through ritual what war gains through force, i.e., societal dominance.)

What follows from the premise are, then, two schools of thought: Those who tend to interpret all forms of behavior in terms of an inescapable genetic code, of which more will be said later. And those who see us as slightly more adaptable, with behavior modified through equal parts of adolescent experience and environmental pressure. In either case, however, the equation is pretty bleak: in the final analysis, we are nothing more than killer apes in the fast lane. If we are occasionally decent, honest and kind, it is simply because we have been so conditioned (on pain of ostracism from the tribe). But those who seek a life of higher meaning are only kidding themselves. Our seventy or so years of survival can actually be measured only in terms of sexual gratification, caloric intake and protection from members of competing tribes, i.e., anyone beyond "the 'hood."

Needless to say, one could theoretically argue that, under such paradigm, criminality is not abnormal at all. Rather, it is simply another way of dealing with the social contract (in much the same way that rogue chimpanzees have been known to exhibit "criminal" behavior when the tribe grows beyond a viable size). But given psychiatric and psychological dependency on state/federal funding, they, too, have made crime a concern.

Traditionally, psychiatric/psychological approach to criminal behavior took two forms, often in conjunction with one another. Drawing upon a grab bag of theory from Pavlovian conditioning to Freudian psychobabble, the psychologist attempted to establish rehabilitative programs, while the psychiatrist experimented with an increasingly wide array of psychotropic drugs. (As a dark footnote to the story, a good many prisoners actually served as unwitting psychiatric guinea pigs for the testing of those drugs, just as prisoners through the 1930s and 1940s had served as unwitting guinea pigs for electroshock and psychosurgical experimentation.) In 1974, however, after a highly controversial study later found to have been quite erroneously conducted, it was determined that no major program could supply proof of efficacy in the rehabilitation of the criminal. Whereupon, the psychologist more or less crept from cells for want of funding, while the psychiatrist commenced doling out drugs with ever more abandon. Today, and notwithstanding continued federal funding of psychiatric research into the genetic and neural sources of criminal behavior—all of which has likewise come to nothing—the rehabilitation of a criminal is still generally viewed as an impossible dream. Instead, the criminal is routinely drugged to keep him tractable but otherwise left to make his own way for better or for worse. Meanwhile, a psychiatric/psychological doctrine that effectively justifies criminality continues to seep into the fabric of society until, as LRH so succinctly puts it, "The psychiatrist and psychologist have carefully developed a lawless and irresponsible public attitude toward crime."

Originally published in 1969, Ron's "Crime and Psychiatry" explores these matters further in blunt detail. ■

CRIME AND PSYCHIATRY

by L. RON HUBBARD

W HEN YOU PUT CRIMINALS in charge of crime, the crime rate rises.

The soaring crime statistics which the police are battling began to rise when the psychiatrist and psychologist moved into the field of education and law.

It used to be that a crime was a crime. When a police officer did his duty, his duty was done.

Now all that has changed. Criminals are "maladjusted" and it is "all society's fault that they are" and the police officer is a beast for daring to interfere with the poor fellows.

The psychiatrist and psychologist have carefully developed a lawless and irresponsible public attitude toward crime.

First and foremost is that Man is just a soulless animal who is not answerable for his own acts. They advertise Man as a push-button stimulus-response robot and claim that only *they* know where the buttons are.

"Underprivileged" people always become criminals, according to these "experts," so the thing to do is make the criminal a privileged being with far more rights than ordinary people.

But the main fault to be found with this psychiatric and psychological influence is that these people only escape the hangman's noose by a fanfare of being above the law themselves.

Crimes of extortion, mayhem and murder are done daily by these men in the name of "practice" and "treatment." There is not one institutional psychiatrist alive who, by ordinary criminal law, could not be arraigned and convicted of extortion, mayhem and murder. Our files are full of evidence on them.

By a mental trick they have hypnotized some politicians into actually believing they are working in "science" and are above the law in that it is necessary that they commit these crimes.

The brutal truth is that these people have not a clue as to what makes the mind work. If they did, they could cure somebody, couldn't they? But they can't and don't. It is obvious, for crime stats have soared since these archcriminals wormed their way into the field of crime.

If you put a complete fake in an engine room to run it, your engine room would soon be a shambles.

This is what has happened in society. Instead of letting the police go about their business, a whole new hierarchy of fake experts has been superimposed on the field.

Thus there is chaos.

If these psychiatrists and psychologists and their "National" Mental Health groups knew their business, then crime statistics would be falling. Naturally. But they are not. Crime statistics, ever since these men have taken over in courts, prisons, education and social welfare, have soared to a point where the honest policeman is near despair.

ANY EXPERIENCED LAW ENFORCEMENT OFFICER KNOWS MORE ABOUT THE CRIMINAL MIND THAN ANY "TWELVE-YEAR-EDUCATED PSYCHIATRIST" OR "SIX-YEAR-EDUCATED PSYCHOLOGIST."

Not the smallest of their crimes is that they absorb all appropriations to rehabilitate people and actively campaign against every church and civic group that used to help with the problem.

But then real top-level criminals wouldn't want the problem of crime to be handled. Would they?

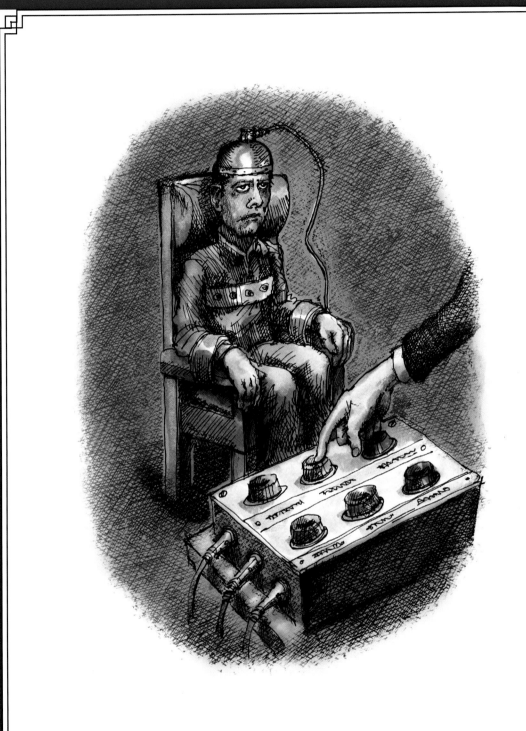

"They advertise Man as a push-button
stimulus-response robot and claim that
only they know where the buttons are."

The Royal Commission of Canada

With the publication of Dianetics: The Modern Science of Mental Health in 1950, and the founding of Scientology two years later, professionals from a variety of fields were seeking L. Ron Hubbard's advice on all sorts of matters pertaining to human interaction. Ron's reply to the Royal Commission of Canada is typical. Noting the remarkably successful use of Dianetics and Scientology in rehabilitating criminal inmates, Canadian legal theorist D. M. Clouston requested an LRH appraisal of Canada's posture on the so-called "insanity defense." Just as typically, Ron's reply is all-embracing. In attempting to redefine criminality as an incurable mental illness, he explains, the psychiatrist has done us another great disservice. Indeed: "The blunt and terrible truth is that so long as insanity can continue to be used as a defense, it will invite criminals into that state of being." ■

L. Ron Hubbard

June 11, 1954

Mr. D. M. Clouston, President
The John Howard Society
St. John's, Newfoundland

My dear Mr. Clouston:

I wish to thank you for your forceful letter on the subject of your testimony as it may be given before a Royal Commission of Canada on the subjects of "Insanity as a Defense" and "Criminal Sexual Psychopaths."

You state that the Royal Commission of Canada has been set up for the purpose of inquiring into and reporting upon two questions:

1. Whether there should be any amendment to the criminal law of Canada relating to "Insanity as a Defense."

2. Whether there should be any amendment to the existing laws of Canada relating to "Criminal Sexual Psychopaths."

As I understand it, you intend to advance the fact that only a trained therapist, with those detectors which may be at his disposal, is competent to make a fair analysis of a person's degree of sanity. And in the second case, you intend that for arbitrary punishment now being imposed, periods of detention should be set during which the prisoner should receive therapeutic treatment (preferably Scientological) and discharged only when found free from the criminal tendencies for which he was detained.

It is very encouraging that a Royal Commission should see fit to inquire into these ranges of justice and it is quite heartening to find that it would invite a man of your caliber to express his views. It may be that something definite may emerge from this and it would appear to be a very hopeful view.

You asked me whether or not I think your approach is sound and invited appropriate suggestions as I may care to make. And I wish to thank you for this opportunity and your courtesy.

In Book Three, Chapter Ten of *Dianetics: The Modern Science of Mental Health,* there is a three-page essay on "Judiciary Dianetics" with which, I believe from your letter, you seem to have some acquaintance.

For whatever they may be worth to you, may I give you my general comments on this matter?

The whole subject of "insanity" in law is adrift, since it is a chip launched into the already-existing definition of criminality. Any confusion as to where to place insanity in law comes about through the basic definition in law itself of insanity and criminality.

Law defines "criminality" more or less as action despite knowledge of right and wrong and "insanity" as an inability to differentiate between right and wrong. If law is based upon the idea that all people are selfish and self-centered, then we can differentiate between criminality and insanity. But if law were to consider Man a social animal, basically it would have to consider that any act which was intentionally harmful would stem from a frame of mind which omitted differentiation of right from wrong. No man, in other words, who was sane in the fullest sense of the word would be motivated by actions which victimized his group or community, since he would realize that he, with the others, would suffer for these activities. And even in a practical sense, it is apparent that the thief, in committing criminal acts, strengthens the necessary force of law in the area and so further inhibits his own freedom.

This is a problem, mainly, of the degree of enlightenment of law itself. It is a matter of what standard the law or the society, the will of which is represented by the law, is willing to recognize—a higher standard of conduct than that enforced by law these many years past. Society is more and more inclined toward the understanding of criminality as "antisocial."

Jurisprudence may content itself to remain with its definition that insanity is the inability to differentiate right from wrong. But this view may be broadened through such inquiries as that of the Royal Commission and by the public's own pressure (which public, actually, such a Commission represents) to account insanity as simply the inability to differentiate.

In the United States certain patterns of thought of recent years have obstructed the growth of justice. Chief amongst these has been a dwelling upon the "criminal mind" as a mind which is strangely distinct and different from the minds of others who are not criminal. But a slightly clearer view should demonstrate that even the "criminal mind" falls within law's own definition for insanity: the inability to differentiate right from wrong. It is obviously wrong for a being to harm his own species, his own group, his own society. Therefore, a being who would commit harmful acts is not differentiating between right and wrong and must at least savor of insanity.

Here we have a problem of "where to draw the line." At what point does an individual cease to be sane and become criminal? At what point, then, does he cease to be criminal and become insane? Custom, from which law itself was born, has long proposed the solution to this problem in its own definition for insanity.

In order to classify criminals, we would have to classify crime. We would discover that crime was subdivided into accidental and intentional crime. Society punishes crime only when it considers the crime to be intentional. If the crime is intentional, then the intent also included the intention of harming the society. Thus a criminal action, by a broad sweep, could be said to be an insane action—and all within the definition of law itself. It could be defined that when a man descends to intentionally harmful action against his fellow, he has descended at least into the upper band of insanity. Law could cleave open a path for itself by applying the classification of "insane" to criminals. In view of the fact that past systems of punishment have not reformed criminality or abated it, law seems more inclined to take this view and *would* take it could it be demonstrated to them that this inability to differentiate right from wrong could be altered to the betterment of society. As prison systems have been found to produce even more hardened criminality than they have remedied, it is entirely possible that law might comfortably entertain a change of view on the subject and treat criminals for what they are: mentally deranged persons.

With this other choice, law finds itself often betrayed. That choice is the permitting of criminals to escape law by reason of "insanity." If a criminal is proven insane, he is permitted, at least to some degree, to escape the penalty which would ordinarily be incurred by his act. Law, by retaining this segregation, defeats its own ends and deprives itself of its prey. Only in the face of an almost complete misunderstanding of insanity could the people engaged in government be persuaded that the label "insane" should permit criminals to escape punishment. Thus, to that degree, insanity itself seems to be feared and is tolerated.

The blunt and terrible truth is that so long as insanity can continue to be used as a defense, it will invite criminals into that state of being. Further, such laws as provide an escape from punishment thus unharness the energies of many against their fellow men who would otherwise be curbed. For example, a slightly insane person, by reason of his "mental state," might feel it unnecessary to obey law which actually was within his full understanding. It is far from right that law should provide an escape for the guilty on such grounds.

By concentrating its attention upon the fact that insanity, if proven, will permit a person to escape justice, law is overlooking the fact that crime apparently stems uniformly from an inability to differentiate to a degree which a sane man would ordinarily consider sane. Law is faced with the enigma of insanity as a means of thwarting justice and thus insanity must continually be disproven in the field of criminality, whereas it is time that criminality be proven to be insanity. I have worked with many criminals and have been, in order to observe criminality, a police officer for a short time. And it is my very close observation that anyone subject to criminal tendencies is, in a much broader sense, insane and that his insanity reaches much wider than the field of crime, but invades hallucination, persecution and mental disabilities, which are in themselves symptoms of insanity.

The insanity of the criminal has its incidence in a conviction that the first group, the family, has no function or need for him and develops upon the recognition that the society does not want him. This is apparently the genus of that antisocialness we call criminality. The insanity is further developed by continuous association with others who are of the same conviction and who form groups, which groups are motivated by a need for revenge against the society. Current methods of punishment and police handling only deepen this conviction. And it can be said, so far as jail sentences are concerned, that the more punishment a criminal receives, the more insane he becomes on the very subject of his criminality. Thus the society victimizes itself by bringing from the realm of delusion into the starkness of reality the fact that the individual is not wanted by any of his fellows, save a few of his most intimate associates. By joining hands in their thirst for revenge against the society which rejects them, these criminals then form societies of their own. And the final result of this dwindling spiral is the deterioration of the society as a whole under duress of laws which, seeking to repress the few, suppress the many. Without such criminal gangs, people such as Hitler, who depended utterly upon them for his ascent to power, would themselves be powerless. Thus the subject of criminality moves intimately into the field of government.

We might find then that insanity should be prohibited as a defense, but that at the same time all criminality defined as intentional harm against the society should be classified as a greater or lesser extent of insanity and that the criminal should be, as you suggest, uniformly detained for treatment. And we find also, as we examine this problem and see the disastrous effects of early and unqualified releases from prison upon the society, that a criminal should be detained until it could be ascertained with great certainty that he would not further victimize the society. This last strikes directly at the parole system, which is an unhappy one at best, and would make it the complete responsibility of parole boards to insure the society against further criminal acts on the part of the released prisoner.

In the absence of a remedying treatment and practical means to effect it, such a course as this would be considered inhuman in the extreme. Even a hardened judge might recoil from the idea that insanity should never be used as a defense and from the intention to incarcerate criminals for their lifetime, if necessary, to insure society against their depredations. These are very strong measures.

Today, however, several experiments have demonstrated that treatment for criminality can be administered at very little cost to the state. This cost is as small as a few cents per prisoner. By means of Group Processing, a great deal has been done in this field. The treatment itself is administered by magnetic tape recordings. The problem could not have been solved as long as individual application of therapy remained a necessity by reason of technology. But with the advance of Group Processing, the majority of criminals could be rehabilitated and freed by parole boards, using sanity as their criteria, without injury to the society. Even though this processing would not be effective upon all criminals to which it was administered, according to present standards and practices, it would at least be effective upon the majority.

With regard to the second part of the purposes of the Royal Commission of Canada, it is my own opinion that laws relating to "Criminal Sexual Psychopaths" should be no different from laws relating to other criminalities. For the sexual psychopath, as Sigmund Freud long ago recognized, is a mentally ill person.

In both these matters, we find the law capable of advancing to the degree that it is willing to accept its responsibility to the society at large. It is the purpose and function of law to safeguard the citizens of the society against the depredations or criminal practices of the few. If the law is totally responsible, it would act to totally insure the citizenry against crime. This cannot be done by suppression of the citizenry at large, for this is the regulation of the many to monitor the few.

Even without Scientology, without adopting its practices, law could be far more effective in safeguarding the society as a whole simply by reclassifying what it means by "criminal" and firmly observing its own definition for "insane." With Scientology, once it has segregated out the criminals and the insane, once it has made its purpose distinct and clear, its detention of criminals until they were once more social could be resolved by the administration of tested processes to the criminals and the release of those who had responded on a group level. This, however, is a very long view and is far too firm a stand to expect from the judiciary, as these cannot but go by the customs of the people whom they serve. A long mile could be commenced upon this road, however, by demonstrating that groups of prisoners detained in prisons could undergo individual change by a rearrangement of their ideas and by releasing those so benefited into the society and by tracing their course until it was firmly established whether or not they had become social. With this step and with the evidence thus brought into being, it might very well follow that a broad evolution in law would ensue.

I wish to thank you very much for writing me. I hope you will let me hear more about this, as I am intensely interested.

My very best,
L. Ron Hubbard

The Solution to a MODERN MORAL CRISIS

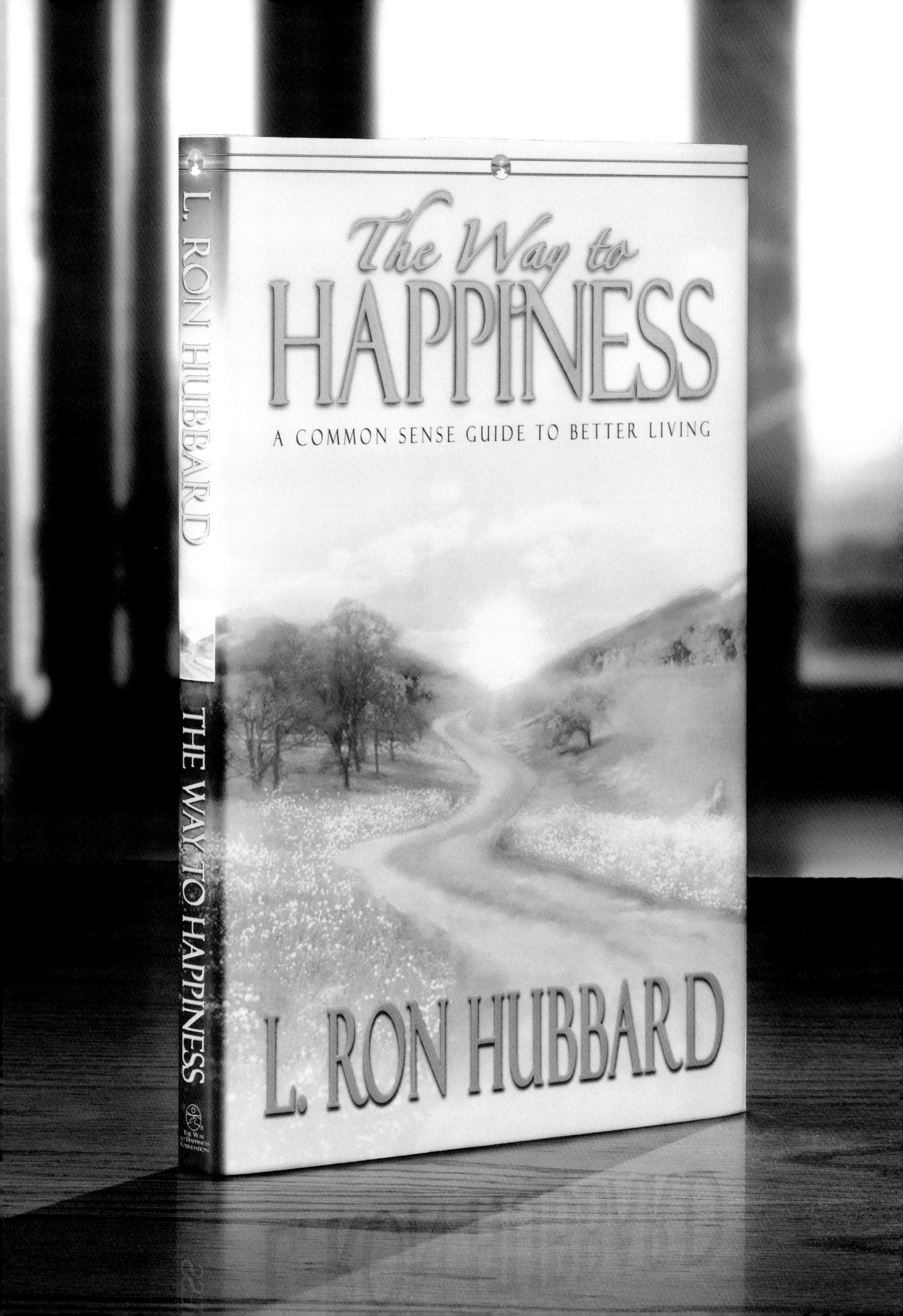

The Way to
HAPPINESS
A COMMON SENSE GUIDE TO BETTER LIVING
L. RON HUBBARD
L. RON HUBBARD
THE WAY TO HAPPINESS

The Solution to a
Modern Moral Crisis

IN 1973, AFTER AN ABSENCE OF SOME TWELVE YEARS, RON returned to the United States for an extended stay in New York City. His mission was sociological and, more simply: to reacquaint himself with a nation comprising the bulk of his readers. To that end, he literally immersed himself in an urban sprawl, and what he found proved most disturbing. Among notes from the period are several references to what he described as "the depowering" of the human spirit and an urge towards "oblivion" in an absence of hope. While in later conversation, he spoke of a cultural crisis the likes of which had not been seen since fourth-century Rome. Yet when eventually asked to sum up his impressions of life in Manhattan circa 1973, he very simply and evocatively replied that he felt as if "on an island that had been destroyed by some superior force."

The analogy is apt, and if causes have long been debated, the statistics are inarguable: Since 1960 (the year following Ron's departure from the United States) violent crime—most of it drug related—had risen more than 250 percent. Through the same period, divorce rates had doubled, illegitimate births had commensurately swelled, while teenage suicide had risen yet another 360 percent. Then there was what could not be statisticized, but was finally just as tangible: "Somebody even had noticed it and wrote a song about it," Ron explained, "My Town Is Dead."

He drew no summary conclusions and, in fact, he twice asks rhetorically in later conversation, "This culture—what the hell has happened to it?" (While adding, as if to himself, "Something...") Nevertheless, his New York notes, comprising several pages of initial observations, would definitely seem to offer a clue. In the first place, he writes, "Suppression can be rampant when there is no code of right conduct. All behavior can thus be declared accusatively wrong or doubtful, and

The first moral code based wholly on common sense, *The Way to Happiness* provides a universal guide to living applicable to all peoples in all cultures

harassment and individual uncertainty can result." He then pointedly considers parallels between diminished church attendance and the proliferation of pornography, while once again noting: "Oblivion is more sought than a hereafter." Hence the rise of alcohol and drug abuse. Finally, and herein lay the string he would continue to pull for some time to come:

"When religion is not influential in a society or has ceased to be, the state inherits the entire burden of public morality. It then must use punishment and police. Yet this is unsuccessful, as morality not inherent in the individual cannot be enforced with any great success...

"There must be more reason and more emotional reasons to be moral than threat of human discipline."

Thereafter, he continued to address the problem on several fronts: with the development of a Scientology drug rehabilitation program (ultimately to prove the world's most successful); with the continued encouragement of Scientology Ethics Technology for the rehabilitation of criminal populations; and—noting the correlation between illiteracy and criminality—with the implementation of Scientology learning tools in the secular arena. But what he increasingly saw as the underlying

moral crisis—that returns us to the central problem of psychiatric and psychological influence.

"What will men do when they believe that they are only mud?" he asked from his Southern California home in 1981. Then significantly adds: "Taught to believe he is but a beast, he is now becoming convinced that he is the helpless victim of his own passions." What had led him to that statement was a trail of research picked up in 1976 upon his resettlement in the United States—and specifically the steady proliferation of what he referred to as a new "Man-from-mud" onslaught, but is more generally known as either evolutionary psychology or New Social Darwinism.

The roots are dark and factually wind right through Third Reich theories of racial purity and the liquidation of inferiors. While more recently, a New Darwinian gospel fostered obscene comparisons between homicide rates within African-American communities and violence within overpopulated baboon communities. (And, of course, who can forget Harvard sociobiologist Edward O. Wilson's inflammatory remarks concerning the evolutionary behavior parallels between humans and termites.) But even darker still is the final construct of this evolutionary psychology, the dangling conclusion of what LRH dubbed a "worship of the atom."

The LRH answer, from the autumn of 1980, was *The Way to Happiness.* In a preliminary word, he spoke of the moral code

"The ties that held men together as Mankind and made them honorable have been sundered by an onslaught of false materialism."

In a sentence the premise is this: If Man is but a soulless sum of his genetic heritage, sprung from "primordial pond scum," as the New Darwinists themselves have put it, then all he feels and does is likewise but a product of genetics. If he loves, it is because he is genetically programed to love for the propagation of the race. If he fears, he is similarly only responding to some innate genetic code. And however socially or politically complex the circumstances, if he kills, he is likewise only acting out an ingrained genetic urge. Needless to say, more than one homicide defense has been mounted under a New Darwinist banner that effectively says, "It was all in the genes."

And when one distills all *that* to an essence in what Ron dubbed "the holy test tube," the message becomes this: if Man is too often immoral, it's because there is ultimately no morality beyond survival of the fittest by tooth and claw.

as a traditional guideline for social accord. If such traditional covenants no longer seemed wholly relevant to a post-Biblical world, they had served well enough for the time. Case in point are the Ten Commandments, reflective of a nomadic existence cemented by devotion to one God. Hence the first commandment: "Thou shalt have no other gods before me." Likewise, and however seemingly irrelevant today, the prohibition against graven images, the taking of the Lord's name in vain and a strict observance of the Sabbath all worked to knit a tribal community with intense piety. Then, too, because Mosaic Code is essentially an article of faith, it continued to remain in force only so long as faith remained—or to bring the argument full circle—until usurped by a materialistic doctrine and what amounts to a purely biological code: *If we need it, take it; if it feels good, do it; and if we feel threatened, then either flee or kill it.*

In truly specific and alarming ways, then, LRH declared, "Old social values have been broken. New moral values have not replaced them. The world of cultural dignity today is in a state of disintegration. The ties that held men together as Mankind and made them honorable have been sundered by an onslaught of false materialism." He then went on to very correctly point out that, relevant or not, traditional religious influences were fast waning, and specifically referenced a United States Supreme Court decision that effectively banned the teaching of the Ten Commandments. Consequently, he concluded, "People and even little kids in schools have gotten the idea that high moral standards are a thing of the past," which, in turn, brought him to the pivotal question: "What if one were to put out a *nonreligious* moral code? One that appealed to the public. One that would be popular and could be kept. One that would increase the survival potential of the individual amongst his fellows. And one the general public itself would pass on."

The first moral code based wholly upon common sense, *The Way to Happiness* offers twenty-one precepts for life in what has become a cynical and largely faithless age. The appeal is entirely logical. Each precept marks the edge of a road to better survival and happiness for oneself and one's fellows. In that regard, *The Way to Happiness* becomes an actual code for living—a technology if you will. Thus, for example, one is advised to be temperate and abstain from harmful drugs, not on principle, but because that road to happiness cannot be walked unless one is physically able to enjoy life. Likewise, one is cautioned against promiscuity not arbitrarily, but because relationships and families will shatter in the face of infidelity. With the same logic, readers are enjoined to live with truth and bear no false witness, as "There is nothing unhappier than one who tries to live in a chaos of lies." His injunction against the criminal act is also a matter of unarguable reasoning. Those who commit crimes, whether apprehended or not, he writes, "are yet weakened before the might of the state." Then, too, of course, there can be no happiness if one murders or is himself murdered.

There is more, including precepts pertaining to the care of children, honoring one's parents, safeguarding our environment, supporting those of good will and fulfilling obligations. Additionally included for each precept is a note on *application,* as in the LRH advice to practice for the sake of gaining competence and encourage others to be industrious. While continuing throughout is that very key and very potent central truth: survival, and thus our happiness, is inextricably linked to all dynamics.

The dissemination of this booklet alone, Ron tells us, can factually change the fabric of this civilization. It can actually usher in "a new era for human relations." If the statement seems overly optimistic, with well over a hundred million copies now in circulation, it is not. Although cumulative effects are difficult to gauge (for how can one measure tolerance and decency with the same statistical accuracy as murder rates?), as succeeding pages will bear out, we are honestly witnessing what may be described as miraculous. ∎

The twenty-one precepts of *The Way to Happiness* may be likened to the edges of a road. For those who know where those edges lie, that road becomes a smooth and fast highway. To plainly mark those edges, the eighty pages of the booklet offer a full explanation of each precept and its application in everyday life. Excerpted below is Ron's introduction to the booklet and the simple statement of the precepts themselves.

Moral Precepts from
The Way to Happiness

1. TAKE CARE OF YOURSELF.

2. BE TEMPERATE.

3. DON'T BE PROMISCUOUS.

4. LOVE AND HELP CHILDREN.

5. HONOR AND HELP YOUR PARENTS.

6. SET A GOOD EXAMPLE.

7. SEEK TO LIVE WITH THE TRUTH.

8. DO NOT MURDER.

9. DON'T DO ANYTHING ILLEGAL.

10. SUPPORT A GOVERNMENT DESIGNED AND RUN FOR ALL THE PEOPLE.

11. DO NOT HARM A PERSON OF GOOD WILL.

12. SAFEGUARD AND IMPROVE YOUR ENVIRONMENT.

13. DO NOT STEAL.

14. BE WORTHY OF TRUST.

15. FULFILL YOUR OBLIGATIONS.

16. BE INDUSTRIOUS.

17. BE COMPETENT.

18. RESPECT THE RELIGIOUS BELIEFS OF OTHERS.

19. TRY NOT TO DO THINGS TO OTHERS THAT YOU WOULD NOT LIKE THEM TO DO TO YOU.

20. TRY TO TREAT OTHERS AS YOU WOULD WANT THEM TO TREAT YOU.

21. FLOURISH AND PROSPER.

English

Aceh

Afrikaans

Albanian

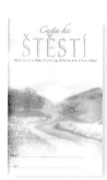

Czech

Danish

Dari Farsi

Icelandic

Igbo

Ilocano

Indonesian

Italian

Malagasy

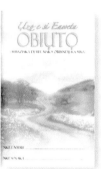

Malay

Maori

Mongolian

Ndebele

Slovenian

Somali

Spanish Castilian

Spanish Latin American

Swahili

Amharic

Arabic

Armenian

Basque

Belorussian

Bengali

Dutch

Ewe

Farsi

Filipino

Finnish

French

Japanese

Jawa Kromo

Kannada

Kapampangan

Kazakh

Khmer

Nepalese

Nigerian Pidgin

Northern Sotho

Norwegian

Pangasinan

Pashto

Swedish

Tagalog

Tamil Indian

Tamil Malaysian

Thai

Tigrigna

HAPPINESS

by L. RON HUBBARD

TRUE JOY AND HAPPINESS are valuable.

If one does not survive, no joy and no happiness are obtainable.

Trying to survive in a chaotic, dishonest and generally immoral society is difficult.

Any individual or group seeks to obtain from life what pleasure and freedom from pain that they can.

Your own survival can be threatened by the bad actions of others around you.

Your own happiness can be turned to tragedy and sorrow by the dishonesty and misconduct of others.

I am sure you can think of instances of this actually happening. Such wrongs reduce one's survival and impair one's happiness.

You are important to other people. You are listened to. You can influence others.

The happiness or unhappiness of others you could name is important to you.

Without too much trouble, using this book, you can help them survive and lead happier lives.

While no one can guarantee that anyone else can be happy, their chances of survival and happiness can be improved. And with theirs, yours will be.

It is in your power to point the way to a less dangerous and happier life.

Chavacano

Chinese

Chinese Traditional

Creole

Croatian

Hausa

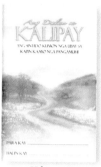
Hebrew

Hiligaynon

Hindi

Hungarian

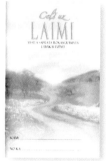
Latvian

Lithuanian

Macedonian

In striking evidence of its universal appeal are *The Way to Happiness* editions in better than one hundred languages

Samoan

Serbian

Sinhalese

Siswati

Slovak

Vietnamese

Waray-Waray

Xhosa

Yoruba

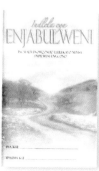
Zulu

Bicolano   Bosnian   Bulgarian   Burmese   Catalan   Cebuano

     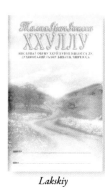

Galician   Georgian   German   Greek   Guarani   Gujarati

Kinyarwanda   Kirundi   Korean   Kyrgyz   Laotian   Lakskiy

Polish   Portuguese   Portuguese Brazilian   Punjabi   Romanian   Russian

Tigrinya   Turkish   Turkmen   Ukranian   Urdu   Uzbek

    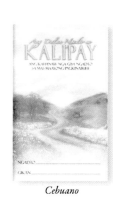

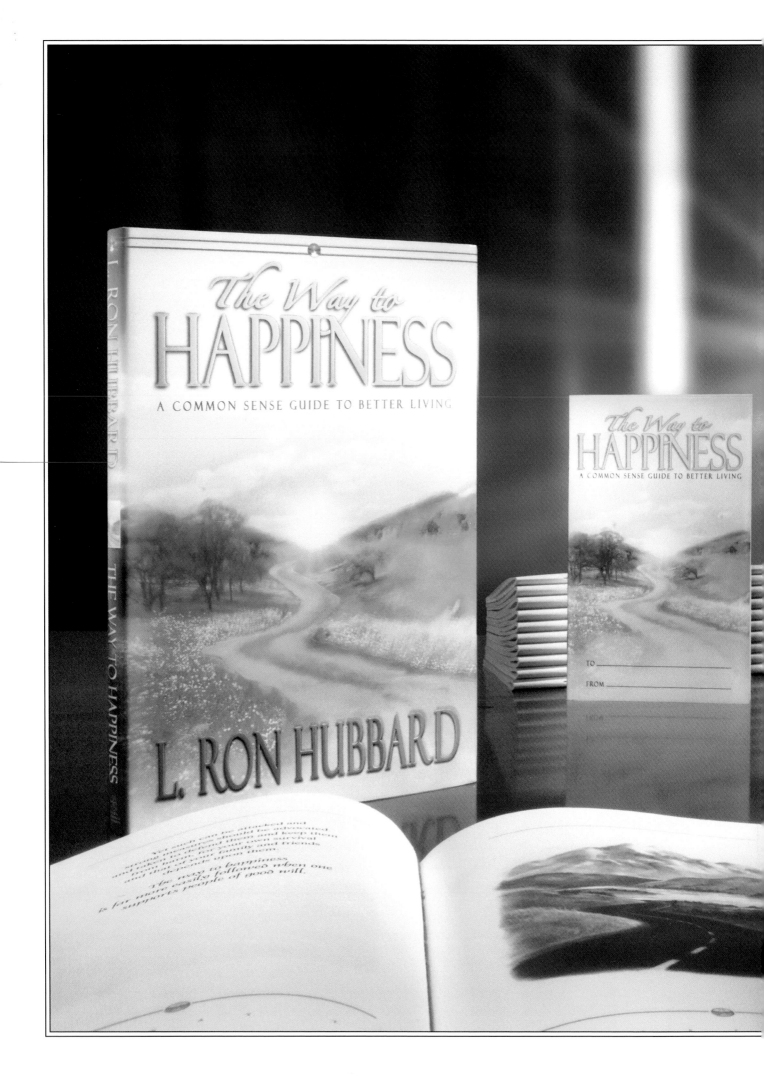

Visually presenting the twenty-one precepts—complete and unabridged—is *The Way to Happiness* book on film. With a multicultural story line to dramatize the precepts, it is designed to reach diverse peoples for which *The Way to Happiness* was always intended. Thus the alienated child, the disenfranchised teenager, the fallen mother, wayward father, not to mention the everyday citizen—all may now appreciate *The Way to Happiness* with a depth that only an audiovisual medium makes possible.

The Way to Happiness Foundation International in Glendale, California, where global distribution
is coordinated across more than two hundred nations to better than one hundred million people

CHAPTER FIVE

The Way to HAPPINESS FOUNDATION

The Way to Happiness Foundation

SINCE ORIGINAL PUBLICATION OF *THE WAY TO HAPPINESS* IN 1981, response has been immediate and remarkable. In the main, distribution is grass-roots and accomplished through sponsorship and coordination with The Way to Happiness Foundation in Glendale, California. Typically, bundles of booklets are donated on

behalf of businesses, schools, civic bodies, youth groups, social service agencies, police and military organizations. Booklets are further distributed in classic hand-to-hand fashion wherein individuals present *The Way to Happiness* to friends and associates who, in turn, present copies to others. In that way, the booklets circulate throughout neighborhoods and communities precisely in accord with that LRH metaphor *"The pebble, dropped in a pool, can make ripples to the furthest shore."* Reflecting the same are booklets with customized covers bearing personal messages, names and logos of every description—from professional and corporate offices to civic governments and law enforcement agencies, from nationally celebrated athletes and performers to prime ministers and presidents. The LRH point here:

"It is in your power to point the way to a less dangerous and happier life."

Likewise reflecting the statement are various youth-based projects providing young adults with opportunities to demonstrate such precepts as "Safeguard and Improve Your Environment" and "Set a Good Example." Meanwhile Way to Happiness essay contests and reading programs further engage tens of thousands of schools and many millions of students. Moreover, those who would imagine such contests might fall flat in this age of sneering cynicism and cool violence are mistaken. To be sure, while virtually all educators note positive changes in attitude among participating students, more than a few reported genuinely dramatic change, e.g., the Tel Aviv school where a Way to Happiness campaign

The Way to Happiness Foundation welcomes anyone with a stake in the moral compass of their communities, including legislators, law enforcement and religious leaders

all but eliminated once rampant schoolyard violence. Similarly, and even more graphically: in the wake of 1992 rioting across Los Angeles, a concerted distribution of *The Way to Happiness* were on the decline and annual homicide rates dropped to zero.

Needless to say, with copies in better than a hundred languages and across some two

"The Way to Happiness is an appropriate prescription—let us have it dispensed in generous doses throughout the world."

was described as a godsend—and not unduly so, as members of notoriously violent gangs were soon seen removing graffiti from 130 buildings. The equally dramatic reduction of crime rates across Hollywood is likewise partly credited to the booklet; hence the precepts displayed on Hollywood Boulevard banners and Los Angeles Police Department editions. Then there was the town in rural Canada where alarming violence levels dropped by more than 85 percent after distribution; and the Harlingen, Texas, "Set a Good Example Contest" providing every city household with *The Way to Happiness,* whereupon crimes of almost every category hundred nations, there is much, much more. Introduced into a deeply troubled Colombia in the early 1990s, the booklet soon saw broad distribution through the efforts of national newspaper chains and a Minister of Education who recommended *The Way to Happiness* to all Colombian educators. Not long thereafter, Colombian police and military agencies adopted the booklet to extraordinary effect. Indeed, and for all intents and purposes, Colombian editions of *The Way to Happiness* went "airborne" in what may only be described as phenomenal ways. To wit: all divisions of the Colombian National Police and all branches

of Colombian military—army, navy, air force and even battle-hardened special forces—all inculcated Way to Happiness programs into cadet-training academies. Moreover, with

hence the subsequent Colombian delegations presenting booklets to sister agencies.

There are similarly coincident correlations between booklet distribution and crime

"If people were put in communication with one another and could give each other a way to happiness, yes, the world would change."

Colombian police and military distribution drives quite literally blanketing the cities with booklets, coupled with continual airing of The Way to Happiness announcements on national television came what was both unprecedented and inconceivable: for the first time in Colombian history, notoriously insidious crime rates were suddenly plummeting. Homicide, kidnapping, carjacking and theft—all precipitously fell to levels not seen in decades until Colombia rightly boasted one of the lowest crime rates in Latin America. Hence the envious neighbors wishing to know how the "Colombian Miracle" came to be; and

reduction across Middle Eastern crisis zones. Pakistan law enforcement topped the index of most corrupted agencies (which is saying a lot). In no small consequence came obscenely soaring crime rates (much of it politically fueled and, in fact, terrorist driven). In reply, and expressly at the behest of a Pakistan Police Inspector General, the International Way to Happiness Foundation initiated precept training seminars in all central academies to some 10 percent of all regional police officers. The net result is another altogether startling addendum to *The Way to Happiness*. In this case: bank robbery, highway robbery, car theft

Right
The Way to
Happiness
Foundation
presents the
twenty-one
precepts in more
than a hundred
languages

and kidnapping—all down by more than 30 percent in a matter of months.

There is an equally pointed story from the Congo, where a Way to Happiness Peace Mission disseminated some twenty thousand booklets among rebel cadres along the Rwandan border. Immediately thereafter, while *New York Times* correspondents report rebel ranks as raptly engrossed with the booklet, warlords appeal to on-the-ground United Nations units for intervention. Then what with booklets similarly presented to opposing troops in Rwanda, a deal was indeed struck and rebels effectively laid down their arms.

There is considerably more from elsewhere across the moral index:

- In the wake of scandalous improprieties, Taiwan's professional baseball league adopted the booklet to regain face with fans.

- Slovakian Gypsies (Roma) similarly embraced the booklet for what is remembered as the "Jasov Miracle"—so named for the fact booklet dissemination inspired a spontaneous cleanup of long-neglected villages and a 40 percent drop in violent crime rates.

- So calming was a distribution of booklets along the West Bank and Gaza Strip, several million copies were summarily requested. Both Hebrew and Arabic translations were provided, while Israelis and Palestinians jointly distributed copies (including military personnel from the former and ministers from the latter). In consequence—and this from a Palestinian General Secretary of Education: "For the first time in my life, I saw many Israeli Jews, young and old, men and women, who risked their own lives to support, help and protect Palestinians."

- Finally, and not to presume more than the facts suggest, it was but two weeks after the dissemination of *The Way to Happiness* in Bosnia (where local newspapers reprinted the text for civilian and military personnel, and the booklet saw broad circulation among diplomatic channels) that three years of negotiations eventually came to fruition with a formal ending of hostilities.

The point, and regardless of how one interprets any single case study: *The Way to Happiness* has repeatedly and dramatically proven itself a force for peace and the reduction of crime. Accordingly, The Way to Happiness Foundation continues to service an ever-broadening movement that indeed suggests a pebble tossed into a pool. Whereupon the circles ripple outward to reach the furthest shore and so all else L. Ron Hubbard declared from the first is fulfilled:

"If people were put in communication with one another and could give each other a way to happiness, yes, the world would change." ∎

Improving Conditions

Improving Conditions

How to Deal with Ups & Down

Confronting & Commu

Criminon

"THERE IS NO REAL REASON WHY THE criminal cannot be detected and also reformed." —L. Ron Hubbard

Thus the first program to utilize his technology toward criminal reform was inaugurated in 1952. It was a modest venture, funded from Ron's lecture fees and manned by volunteers from London's Church of Scientology. It was specifically aimed at juvenile delinquency, then rearing an ugly head in post-war Britain. By 1954, tools drawn from Dianetics and Scientology further proved efficacious in California's Folsom Prison and yet again for the rehabilitation of offenders in Arizona—at which point the stage was set for what we know today as Criminon (without crime).

If all commenced in a then relatively remote New Zealand, the program soon gained fully international momentum. To be sure, a worldwide Criminon office now coordinates LRH rehabilitation tools and *The Way to Happiness* delivery to inmates/parolees in well over fifty nations. In full, the program presents both LRH tools for ethical repair as well as The Way to Happiness Course to help students with practical application of the twenty-one precepts. Given statistical links between illiteracy and criminality, the complete curriculum further includes famed LRH literacy tools for greatly improved reading comprehension, still another battery of LRH technology to help inmates from slipping back to lives of crime and a communication course to help them face life rather than withdraw from it—the very act originally precipitating the criminal condition. Needless to say, the program does not condone psychiatric/psychological methods. Consequently, Criminon enjoys unqualified support from both inmates grown distrustful of psychiatry and correctional officers too frequently bilked by psychologists. Moreover, when the program is installed

Left
Members of a first in-prison rehabilitation program using L. Ron Hubbard's technology, at the Arizona State Prison, 1967

Left The materials of the Criminon program: comprising a road to newfound dignity and self-respect, these courses of study are now delivered in well over a thousand penal institutions across five continents

across entire prison systems, results in terms of lowered recidivism and violence reduction are altogether astonishing.

For example, in what amounted to an early case study of Butler County, Alabama, delinquents, then juvenile-court director and chief probation officer Daniel O. Black had previously reported an 80 percent recidivism rate among paroled or probationed youths. The problem, as Black so succinctly explained:

"There is no real reason why the criminal cannot be detected and also reformed."

"A pair of Nike tennis shoes actually had more value than someone else's life for many of these kids. So it became very apparent that we wouldn't get anywhere unless we could find some way to readjust those values to ones which were more appropriate for society."

In what he then described as an experimental program, copies of the booklet were distributed to inmates or read aloud. The youths were then encouraged to find ways in which the precepts might be applied and, when literacy levels permitted, to compose an essay on each precept. "I could pretend it to be more complex," Black confessed, "but it really is quite simple. I help them with the definition of words they don't understand and otherwise continue to encourage that all-important point of application." Whereupon, as he just as bluntly phrased it: "Results became spectacular." By way of figures, Black went on to report that while regional crime rates had previously escalated on par with national averages, his introduction of *The Way to Happiness* immediately precipitated a *decrease* in crime. Moreover, and even more spectacularly, that 80 percent recidivism rate suddenly fell to but 10 percent.

To what has become a largely hopeless field—with paltry percentages of correctional budgets earmarked for treatment and wardens routinely admitting they can only pass rehabilitation problems on to probation officers—that figure becomes immensely significant. It is even the more so when one recognizes that such success is by no means exclusive to Butler County. "Dramatic" is how yet another juvenile officer described results from the Criminon program at a Los Angeles detention center and cited a marked lessening of hostility, increased willingness to communicate and "extraordinarily, they now feel remorse for what they have done in the past."

Among seemingly incorrigible older felons, results have proven even more dramatic. A notoriously violent Mexican

miraculous. "Yet what speaks even louder," proclaimed South Africa's National Deputy Commissioner of Correctional Services, "is this: not one of those who have done The Way to Happiness program and been released from prison, has since returned."

One could cite many another. At the request of the Rwandan Internal Affairs Ministry, Criminon delivery teams were enlisted to instruct Hutu perpetrators of the 1994 Tutsis

"...not one of those who have done The Way to Happiness program and been released from prison, has since returned."

prison saw 70 percent recidivism rates drop to a negligible fraction after Criminon implementation—and that amidst a virulent cellblock drug trade also ceasing in the wake of LRH technologies. Then there is what those technologies have come to represent within South Africa's supermax prisons: sprawling, imposing and, until the arrival of Criminon, so exceedingly violent they were compared to some perpetually contested "no man's land." It was absolutely not for nothing, then, that a Criminon program reducing cellblock violence to zero was hailed as truly

massacre. Almost immediately thereafter, wardens from five separate compounds were reporting not a single incident of violence in what were previously battlegrounds. Hence descriptions of Criminon as something akin to divine intervention; and hence, Rwandan tribunals for justice and reconciliation suspending sentences for program graduates.

Likewise instituting Criminon across entire prison systems by executive decree is Indonesia. The program features a National Criminon Center for training what are now known as Criminon Rehabilitation Experts

for the fact they can simultaneously work LRH tools and technologies across the full spectrum of correctional institutions—maximum, minimum and supermax security. There is methods employed by the prison system have been utterly ineffective—the upshot of which is the currently high rate of recidivism. The rehabilitative technology employed by

"The Way to Happiness gives you the outcome of your actions.
You understand the outcome of what you do. It's for you."

even a facility now exclusively dedicated to Criminon delivery, while a former Director General of Corrections serves as national program coordinator.

There is considerably more. With sanction from Panama's Presidential Palace, a Criminon pilot was implemented in an altogether hopeless women's facility. Eighteen months later, said facility was so utterly transformed it now stands as a Central American model. Meanwhile and no less definitively, a New York State Department of Correctional Services Captain declares that, "Current

Criminon represents the *only* truly workable means to handle the increasingly burdensome criminal populations."

Again, however, nothing speaks so loudly as the graduates themselves and particularly inasmuch as their message is repeated from so many diverse quarters. (In Poland, to cite yet another, *The Way to Happiness* was reprinted on the prison's own presses.) Yet given where so much of L. Ron Hubbard's work began, it seems only fitting to focus on but one young graduate from the Los Angeles juvenile program. A former member of a neighborhood

gang that once prowled those mean Central Division streets where Ron had walked a beat so many years earlier, his closing words would seem to say everything:

"The Way to Happiness gives you the outcome of your actions. You understand the outcome of what you do. It's for you. It teaches you the Golden Rule. I used to hear about it, but this puts it into perspective. I know what it means now.

"I don't know who this L. Ron Hubbard is, but he is one smart man. If people would just listen to this book, The Way to Happiness, the mass of the people, if they would just understand it, take it, think about it, then the world would be a different place." ■

A few of the thousands of recognitions, proclamations and awards bestowed upon L. Ron Hubbard in acknowledgment of his contributions in the fields of ethics, justice and morality

"Lady Justice"

*Stands as an icon of the Eternal Moral Vector
that's still in our judicial system,
The principle that like a sword stroke on evil steel
Rings and sings psalms of truth and reason
Brings calm things of a just society
to beings free to rise to heights serene.*

Presented to commemorate the centennial celebration of L. Ron Hubbard's birth (1911–2011), and bestows a recognition for his profound contributions in the criminal justice system in the areas of drug rehabilitation and prison reform. These are ongoing social challenges that continue to call for the leadership of vigorous men of intellect the likes of Mr. Hubbard who have inspired individuals to take control of their own lives and influence the lives of others in a positive way.

Honorable Richard B. Sanders
Justice, Washington Supreme Court (retired)

Epilogue

Today, in ways that are actually far more dramatic than reports of criminal mayhem on the six o'clock news, the implementation of L. Ron Hubbard's discoveries are returning men to lives of decency, honor and self-respect. As we have seen, how Ron came to make those discoveries is likewise a far more dramatic achievement than the passage of new crime bills or the erection of new prisons. But what is ultimately most dramatic of all, is the vision that allowed him to pave that road to honor and self-respect. It is probably best summarized in a 1956 lecture entitled "The Deterioration of Liberty," wherein he very simply and eloquently proclaimed:

"I admit that some man occasionally will become afraid and will become totally gripped by the belief that there is menace in every fellow man. I admit that a human being can become so aberrated as to constitute a menace to the bulk of the society and that in such a case it is necessary to reacquaint him with society. But I will not admit that there is a naturally bad, evil man on Earth."

APPENDIX

GLOSSARY

A

∞ (infinity symbol): a mathematical symbol that represents infinity. Page 51.

abandon: complete lack of inhibition or self-restraint. Page 68.

abandoned: given up, left off (a habit, practice, etc.); ceased to hold, use or practice. Page 63.

abated: diminished or reduced in intensity, amount, etc. Page 78.

aberrated: subjected to or affected by *aberration*. Page 60.

aberration(s): a departure from rational thought or behavior. From the Latin, *aberrare,* to wander from; Latin, *ab,* away, and *errare,* to wander. It means basically to err, to make mistakes, or more specifically to have fixed ideas which are not true. The word is also used in its scientific sense. It means departure from a straight line. If a line should go from A to B, then if it is "aberrated" it would go from A to some other point, to some other point, to some other point, to some other point, to some other point and finally arrive at B. Taken in its scientific sense, it would also mean the lack of straightness or to see crookedly, as an example, a man sees a horse but thinks he sees an elephant. Aberrated conduct would be wrong conduct, or conduct not supported by reason. Page 11.

able seamen: members of a ship's crew possessing basic skills and qualifications and able to perform routine sea duties. Page 9.

abode: a place where one lives or stays; home. Page 47.

abrogated: done away with something, such as a contract, agreement, law or the like. Page 15.

absolute(s): 1. perfect or complete in quality or nature. Page 52.

2. those things, conditions, etc., that are perfect and complete in quality or nature. Page 56.

abstract: an idea or term considered apart from some material basis or object. Page 1.

abyss: a vast or bottomless opening, void space, etc., thought of as leading to or containing something immensely harmful, destructive, etc. Page 2.

accord: mutual agreement; harmony, with no conflict between two or more people or things. Page 87.

account, expense: the record of an employee's expenses during a particular period. *Pad an expense account* means cheat one's employer by adding false items to an expense account. Page 3.

account (something): regard or consider (something) in a specified way. Page 77.

acquittal: the clearing (of a person) of a charge, as by declaring not guilty. Page 36.

action, hard: fighting between enemy forces that is violent and rough. Page 9.

acute: extremely great or serious. Page 9.

admonishment: a reminder or caution concerning something forgotten or disregarded, as an obligation or a responsibility. Page 30.

adrift: figuratively, off course; drifting with little or no direction. Literally, said of a ship that moves according to the way the wind and water move, if not secured by cables or anchor or if not being pushed by its own power. Page 76.

air: a look, appearance, attitude or manner that expresses some personal quality or emotion. Page 18.

Alabama: a state in the southeastern United States. Page 110.

Alaska: a state of the United States in northwestern North America, separated from the other mainland states by part of Canada. Page 24.

Alcatraz: a maximum-security federal prison formerly used to house extremely dangerous criminals, located on an island of the same name in San Francisco Bay. Originally used as a Spanish fortress and prison, Alcatraz consists of twelve acres of solid rock, is almost constantly enveloped by fog and surrounded by treacherous currents, making escape practically impossible and giving the island its grim reputation. It was used as a prison by the United States Army (1858–1933) and then a federal prison until it closed in 1963. Page 23.

alien: a citizen of a country other than the one in which the person lives or happens to be. Page 45.

alienated: caused to be withdrawn or detached from. Page 99.

all-embracing: covering or applying to all; including everything, without discrimination. Page 74.

alma mater: a school, college or university at which one has studied and, usually, from which one has graduated. Page 23.

alumni: plural of *alumnus,* a graduate or former student of a specific school, college or university. Page 16.

Alvarado: the name of a street in Los Angeles, California. It is named after Juan Bautista Alvarado (1809–1882), Mexican governor of California from 1836 to 1842. The south section of Alvarado Street is situated in a part of the city that has been known for its high crime rate. Page 13.

amassing: gathering for oneself; accumulating (a large amount of something) over a period of time. Page 57.

amount to: develop into; become. Page 20.

analogy: a comparison between two things that are similar in some respects, often used to help explain something or make it easier to understand. Page 18.

Anglo-Saxon, the: any white, English-speaking person, taken as a generalized representative of the Anglo-Saxon people. The term reflects the earlier Germanic tribes, Angles and Saxons, who settled in Britain in the fifth and sixth centuries. Page 23.

antecedent(s): the history, events, characteristics, etc., of one's earlier life. Page 45.

anti-social: hostile to or disruptive of the established social order; of behavior that is harmful to the welfare of people generally. Page 59.

antithetical: directly opposed or contrasted; opposite. Page 9.

apprehended: arrested for having done something illegal. Page 88.

appropriation: a sum of money that has been set aside from a budget, especially a government budget, for a particular purpose. Page 72.

approximates: is similar to something in nature, size or extent. Page 51.

apt: 1. inclined; given to; likely. Page 54.

2. suited to the purpose or occasion; appropriate. Page 85.

aptly: suitably; appropriately. Page 35.

arbitrary: based on judgment or useful selection rather than on the fixed nature of something. Page 50.

archcriminal: the top or leading criminal. *Arch* means chief, most important or most extreme. Page 72.

ardent: intensely devoted, eager or enthusiastic. Page 21.

arena: a sphere of action; field of activity. An *arena* in its literal sense is a central stage, ring, area or the like, used for sports or other forms of entertainment, surrounded by seats for spectators. Page 86.

Arizona: a state in the southwest United States. Page 109.

arraigned: called before a court to answer a criminal charge. Page 71.

array: a large group, number or quantity (of things). Page 3.

arrayed: placed in proper or desired order. Page 18.

article of faith: a basic religious belief held by a group or person. Used with reference to *articles,* the parts of a formal declaration or of a body of rules, beliefs, etc., considered as a whole. Page 87.

aspirant(s): someone who eagerly seeks or hopes to attain something. Page 2.

assert: declare or state emphatically (as being true). Page 42.

Atlanta: a city in and the capital of Georgia, a state in the southeastern United States. Page 3.

atomic: using *atomic energy,* energy that is produced when the central part of an atom (nucleus) splits apart. The pieces of the nucleus then strike other nuclei (centers of atoms) and cause them to split, thus creating a chain reaction accompanied by the release of an immense quantity of energy, such as in an atomic bomb. Page 53.

atonement: satisfaction given for wrongdoing, injury, etc.; amends. Page 33.

attend: take care of; treat. Page 59.

axiomatic: self-evident; obviously true. Page 14.

B

baboon: a large, powerful and aggressive ground-dwelling monkey native to Africa and Asia, with a long snout (resembling that of a dog), large teeth, a short tail, and arms about as long as its legs. Baboons range in weight from 24 pounds (11 kilograms) to 90 pounds (41 kilograms). Page 86.

bail, without: without setting *bail,* a sum of money deposited to secure an accused person's temporary release from custody and to guarantee that person's appearance in court at a later date. *Without bail* means the person must remain in jail and is not permitted even a temporary release. Page 37.

banner: a guiding principle, cause or philosophy, from the literal meaning of *banner,* a flag on a pole, such as one used in battle by a country or a king. Page 87.

barbarism: an absence of culture; uncivilized ignorance marked by wild, violent cruelty. Page 18.

barbarity: brutal or inhuman conduct; cruelty. Page 15.

bar of justice: a partition in a courtroom, beyond which most people may not pass and at which an accused person stands. Page 18.

basic personality: the individual himself. The basic individual is not a buried unknown or a different person, but an intensity of all that is best and most able in the person. Page 11.

basket, heads ready for the: a reference to the executions that occurred during the French Revolution (1789–1799), when thousands of people were beheaded under the guillotine, with a basket made ready to receive the severed heads. Page 39.

batty: insane; crazy. Page 54.

bear false witness: to tell lies or state something false while under oath or in a court of law; to state falsely. *Bear* means to give or provide. *Witness* means swearing to a fact, statement, etc.; proof or evidence. Page 88.

bear out: support, back up or confirm; prove. Page 89.

bedrock: the lowest level; the very bottom. Page 2.

behest: an earnest or strongly worded request. Page 105.

being: a person; an identity. Page 7.

bestow: give or present something to someone. Page 35.

bilked: cheated out of what is due. Page 109.

billy-club: of or relating to a *billy club,* a short stick or club used as a weapon by a police officer. Page 14.

bleated: talked about excessively and pointlessly, likened to making the cry of a sheep or goat. Page 17.

blighting: destroying the promise of; ruining or spoiling. Page 57.

blunt: weaken or impair the strength or force of something. Page 60.

Bosnia: the country officially known as Bosnia and Herzegovina, in southeastern Europe, where civil war occurred in the 1990s. Page 107.

braid: a band or cord on a uniform that shows the rank of the wearer. Page 10.

brass tacks: basic facts; practical details; realities. Page 35.

breaches: violations as of a promise, agreement, rules, etc. Page 33.

breaks faith: violates one's promise or word; acts as a traitor. *Break* means to transgress or violate by disregarding or failing to observe (something); to fail to keep one's word or pledge. *Faith* means a verbal promise, vow or pledge; the duty of fulfilling an obligation. Page 57.

brig: a military slang term for a jail. Originally referring to a jail on board a ship, the term came to be applied as slang for any military or naval prison. Page 9.

broad sweep: a comprehensive view of something; a generalization of a large and diverse group of things or people. Page 77.

Buddhist: of or relating to *Buddhism,* the religion founded by Gautama Siddhartha Buddha (563?–483? B.C.), Indian religious philosopher and teacher. Buddhism emphasizes physical and spiritual discipline as a means of liberation from the physical world. *Buddha* means one who has attained intellectual and ethical perfection by spiritual means. Page 32.

Burks, Arthur J.: (1898–1974) American writer whose enormous output for the pulps included aviation, detective, adventure and horror stories. Page 8.

buzzword: an informal term for a fashionable word or concept, often associated with a particular group of people and not understood by outsiders. Page 2.

C

cadre: a group of activists in a revolutionary organization. Page 106.

caliber: degree of competence, intelligence or ability. Page 76.

caloric: of or pertaining to *calories,* units of energy used as a measurement for the amount of energy that food provides. Page 68.

Calvinistic: of, pertaining to or following the doctrines of Calvinism—the sovereignty of God, the supreme authority of the Scriptures and that certain chosen individuals are predestined to salvation. Page 17.

cap: do more than; exceed. Page 3.

capital: having extremely serious consequences. Page 45.

capital punishment: punishment by death for a crime; death penalty. Page 15.

cartridge(s): a cylindrical case that holds a charge of gunpowder and a bullet and which is put into a gun. Page 13.

causatively: in a manner characteristic of being cause as opposed to effect; originated or produced by one's own efforts; able to cause things effectively. Page 32.

C.C.C.: an abbreviation for *Civilian Conservation Corps,* a former United States Government agency (1933–1942) organized to provide work for the nation's unemployed single young men through developing and preserving the country's natural resources (timber, soil and water). The corps was started during the Great Depression (that period of economic crisis and lowered business activity occurring in the United States from 1929 through most of the 1930s). Participants received job training and engaged in such activities as building roads, flood barriers and dams, planting trees, laying telephone lines, improving parks and fighting forest fires. Page 24.

cellblock: a group of cells (rooms for one or more prisoners) forming a unit in a prison. Page 111.

cemented: united or joined together. Page 87.

Chart of Human Evaluation: a comprehensive chart developed by L. Ron Hubbard that consists of many columns containing the majority of the components of the human mind and all those necessary to process an individual. The chart gives the reaction and behavior of human beings at various levels of aberration and with it one can precisely evaluate and predict human behavior. The Hubbard Chart of Human Evaluation is described in detail in the book *Science of Survival.* Page 31.

Chefoo: an earlier name for *Yantai,* a city and seaport in eastern China. Page 30.

chieftain: the leader or head of a group (often referring to a tribe or clan). Page 17.

chilling: causing a feeling of dread or horror. Page 8.

chip: a small piece (of something) separated from or broken off of something larger. Page 76.

chromosomal: of or having to do with *chromosomes,* rod-shaped structures in the central part (nucleus) of animal and plant cells. Chromosomes carry the genes that supposedly determine sex and the characteristics an organism inherits from its parents. Page 3.

chute, up (down) the: out of (into) a state of failure or ruin, deterioration or collapse. Page 35.

circle, bring full: return to an earlier or first position or situation after leaving it. Page 87.

citizenry: citizens collectively. Page 80.

citizen's arrest: an arrest made by a private citizen if a serious crime is committed in his presence. The authority for such an arrest comes from the fact of being a citizen. Page 12.

civic: of or relating to the duties or activities of citizens in contrast to military, etc.—for example, community organizations or clubs formed to improve life in the community. Page 72.

civil: of legal action involving individual people or groups, as opposed to criminal matters. Page 45.

clean: morally pure; honorable. Page 61.

cleave: make a way into or through something as if by cutting. Page 77.

collective: of or characteristic of a group of individuals taken together. Page 20.

come to grief: suffer misfortune or ruin. Page 63.

commensurately: in a manner that corresponds in size or degree to something else; proportionately. Page 2.

commissioned: (of a warship) readied for active service by being equipped, manned and under command. *Commissioned for submarine defense* refers to being readied for active service as a *submarine defense vessel,* a warship capable of defending an area against attack by enemy submarines. Page 11.

commissioner: a government official or representative in charge of a department or district. Page 111.

compass: literally, a device for finding directions, usually with a magnetized needle that automatically points to the north. Hence, figuratively, something that helps one find the correct course of action. Page 103.

compelling: exerting a strong and irresistible effect, influence, etc. Page 67.

compensatory: serving to offset the negative effects or results of something else. Page 46.

complement: add to in a way that enhances or improves. Page 32.

compounded: increased, added to or intensified. Page 62.

computation: of or relating to calculating or processing of data (to come up with answers); of thinking. Page 53.

concentric: having a common center; used to describe circles that lie one within another. Page 51.

concerted: jointly arranged or carried out. Page 104.

condition: in Scientology Ethics, a *condition* is a state of operation. An organization or its parts or an individual passes through various states of existence. These, if not handled properly, bring about shrinkage and misery and worry and death. If handled properly, they bring about stability, expansion, influence and well-being. Each condition has an exact sequence of steps, called a *formula,* which one can use to move from the current condition to another, higher and more survival condition. Page 1.

Congressional: of or pertaining to *Congress,* the elected group of politicians that is responsible for making the law in the United States. It consists of two parts: the House of Representatives (the lower of the two lawmaking bodies) and the Senate (the higher of the two). Page 46.

Conservatism: an ideology or political philosophy based on the tendency to preserve what is established and existing; the inclination to limit change. Page 30.

Constitution: a document containing the fundamental laws of the United States that was put into effect on 4 March 1789. It establishes the form of the national government and defines the rights and liberties of the American people. Page 37.

constitution: the system of fundamental principles and laws according to which a nation is governed. Page 44.

construct: an idea or theory, especially a complex one formed from a number of simpler elements. Page 87.

contemplative: involving or expressing *contemplation,* long and attentive consideration of something. Page 1.

content itself: accept as adequate despite wanting more or better. Page 77.

contrived: planned or schemed; managed. Page 18.

convention: a rule, method or principle of conduct established through long usage and accepted by society; custom. Page 17.

conviction: firmly held belief or opinion; the state of being convinced (as of the truth or rightness of one's belief or acts). Page 79.

convict labor: work imposed upon criminals in addition to imprisonment. Page 37.

cool: calmly and deliberately shameless or bold. Page 103.

coon: an offensive term for a black person. Page 42.

core: central or basic. Page 11.

corollary: a situation, fact, etc., that is the natural and direct result of another one. Page 11.

coroner: an official who is responsible for investigating the deaths of people who have died in a sudden, violent or unusual way. Page 8.

corporal: a low-ranking officer in various armed forces. Page 23.

corvette: a lightly armed, fast ship used especially during World War II (1939–1945) to accompany a group of supply ships and protect them from attack by enemy submarines. Page 9.

couched: expressed in a particular style or with a particular choice of words. Page 18.

court, high: any court that has general power or authority over other courts and can hear and decide on cases from them. Page 45.

court, low: a court whose decisions are subject to review or to appeal to a higher court; the court that first hears or tries cases. Page 45.

court-martialed: brought before a *court-martial,* a trial by a military or naval court of officers appointed by a commander to try persons for offenses under military law. Page 10.

court, upper: any court that can hear and decide on cases from other courts; a court of appeals. Page 37.

covenants: the conditional agreements made by God to humanity, such as the agreement between God and the ancient Israelites, in which God promised to protect them if they observed His law and were faithful to Him. Page 87.

covetous: having a strong desire to possess something, especially something that belongs to another person. Page 57.

crack: excelling in skill or achievement; first-rate. Page 9.

creation: the world and everything in it. Page 14.

credentials: evidence that confirms someone's position or status, such as a badge, letter or other official identification. Page 12.

creed: a system or set of religious beliefs or opinions. Page 45.

"Criminal Sexual Psychopaths": a psychiatric label assigned to someone who, having committed a sexual offense (such as rape, child molestation, indecent exposure and the like), is committed to a psychiatric facility for "treatment," rather than going to jail, on the basis that he is suffering from a mental disorder coupled with criminal inclination to commit such sexual offenses. Page 75.

critical: having a decisive importance in the success or failure of something. Page 14.

crowning: representing a level of supreme achievement, attainment, etc. Page 32.

crying: demanding immediate attention or remedy; critical; severe. Page 20.

Cullavagga: Buddhist scriptures that lay out rules of conduct for Buddhist monks and procedures for addressing offenses within the monastic community. Page 32.

cunning: the use of skill and cleverness in a way that is intended to deceive. Page 20.

curbed: restrained, controlled or checked. Page 78.

curriculum: a course of study in a particular subject or area of activity. Page 3.

cutthroat: one likely to cut throats; a very aggressive, dangerous person. Page 2.

cutting (their brother's / one's own) throat(s): bringing about (another's or one's own) ruin or downfall. Page 57.

cynical: characterized by a disbelief in human sincerity or goodness and a bitter distrust in people. Page 88.

D

dangling: characterized by being indefinite or uncertain. Page 87.

dark: characterized by evil or wickedness. Page 12.

dark, in the: in ignorance; uninformed. Page 18.

Darwin: Charles Darwin (1809–1882), English naturalist and author. His book *On the Origin of Species* proposed a theory to explain evolution of life forms to higher forms. Page 67.

Darwinism, New Social: *Social Darwinism* was a nineteenth-century theory that human societies and races follow the same biological laws of natural selection as plants and animals. *Natural selection* is the process, according to English biologist Charles Darwin (1809–1882), whereby organisms better adapted to their environment tend to survive and produce more offspring. In the 1960s and 1970s, *New Social Darwinism* picked up the earlier theory, attempting to show that intelligence and behavior are determined by genetics rather than by cultural influences, thus indicating that some societies or races are more advanced than others because their members are biologically superior. Page 86.

dawn man: any prehistoric type of man, now extinct. Page 17.

decamp: leave a place abruptly or secretly; run away. Page 42.

decree: a formal and authoritative order, especially one having the force of law. Also, the issuance of such an order. Page 46.

decried: strongly disapproved of, openly criticized or condemned. Page 34.

defaulted: failed to meet an obligation when required or expected, especially a financial one. Page 20.

degrees, overburdened by: having an excessive number of *degrees,* academic titles given by universities and colleges. A degree indicates the completion of a course of study. Page 18.

Democracy: a system of government in which power is given to the people, who rule either directly or through freely elected representatives, and which is characterized by tolerance and freedom of expression. Page 30.

Denver: capital city of the state of Colorado, in the western United States. Page 3.

deploring: feeling or expressing strong disapproval of. Page 18.

depowering: removing or taking the ability or strength (power) away from. Page 85.

depredation(s): the act of attacking and preying upon. Page 80.

depression: a period of drastic decline in the national economy, characterized by decreasing business activity, falling prices and unemployment. The best known of such periods is the Great Depression, which occurred in the 1930s. Page 53.

deprivation: the act of taking something away from somebody or preventing somebody from having something. Also, the state of being without or denied something, especially of being without adequate food or shelter. Page 37.

depth charge: a large can filled with explosive material designed to sink and explode at a certain depth, used to destroy submarines. Page 10.

deranged: disordered; especially disordered in mind; crazy; insane. Page 11.

dereliction: deliberate or conscious neglect; negligence; delinquency. Page 10.

descend (to): behave in a way that is below normal standards. Page 33.

descent: the established connection between an individual and his ancestors or the race, ethnic group or region from which he or she comes. Page 45.

despoiling: destroying or stripping away the value or worth of something; making something worthless or useless. Page 32.

detention center: also called *juvenile hall,* a holding center for juvenile delinquents (young persons not more than a specified age, usually eighteen years, who habitually break the law). It is a secure facility for those who are usually awaiting court hearings and/or placement in long-term disciplinary-care programs for committing juvenile crimes, such as drug possession or robbery. Juveniles are typically held in a detention center to ensure appearance in court, as well as for public safety reasons. Page 111.

devoid: completely lacking in or without something. Page 30.

Dianetics: Dianetics is a forerunner and substudy of Scientology. Dianetics means "through the mind" or "through the soul" (from Greek *dia,* through, and *nous,* mind or soul). Dianetics is further defined as what the mind or soul is doing to the body. Page 1.

diploma, high-school: an official document given by a high school, indicating that somebody has completed a course of education or training and reached the required level of competence. In the United States, a *high school* is a school consisting of grades 9 through 12, or sometimes grades 10 through 12. (A *grade* is a class or year in a school.) A student is normally about fifteen years old when he starts high school and about eighteen years old when he graduates. Page 16.

diplomatic channels: routes of communication among or involving *diplomats,* people who represent the interests of their own country by living and working in other countries to maintain political, economic and social relations. Page 107.

discernment: the act of distinguishing; perception of the difference between things. Page 51.

disenfranchised: removed from or deprived of a right, membership, pleasure, etc. Page 99.

dished out: given out; distributed. Page 14.

distills: creates something from the essential or most important elements of something larger or longer. Page 87.

doctrine: a particular principle, position or policy taught or advocated by some political, scientific or philosophic group. Page 69.

doling out: distributing something. Page 68.

"Donald Duck" navy: after the attack on Pearl Harbor by the Japanese (7 December 1941), many Americans joined the US Navy and the Coast Guard Reserve. Often they were assigned to newly constructed submarine chasers, patrol craft, gunboats, tugboats, converted yachts and other small craft. During World War II (1939–1945), most of these craft never had names, only numbers, and the crew members of this fleet of small craft dubbed it the "Donald Duck" navy. Page 10.

dope: illegal drugs. Page 59.

dossier: an accumulation of records, reports, pertinent data and documents bearing on a single subject of study or investigation. Page 10.

draw the line: lay down a definite limit of action. Page 77.

driven: forced (someone or something) into a particular state or condition, often an extremely negative one. Page 62.

drive(s): 1. any of the inner urges that stimulate activity, energy and initiative. Page 49.

2. an organized effort to achieve a particular purpose. Page 105.

drive (something) home: make a point strongly or firmly. *Drive,* in this case, means press or urge onward; bring about by urgency or pressure. *Home* here means to the vital center or seat; to the very heart or root of the matter. Page 9.

dubbed: gave a descriptive name to something; called. Page 87.

duress: pressure, such as force or threats, to make somebody act or think in a certain way against his will or better judgment. Page 79.

dwelling upon: spending time upon or lingering over (a thing) in action or thought; remaining with the attention fixed on. Page 77.

dwindling spiral: the worse someone (or something) gets, the more capacity he has to get worse. *Spiral* here refers to a progressive downward movement, marking a relentlessly deteriorating state of affairs, and considered to take the form of a spiral. The term comes from aviation, where it is used to describe the phenomenon of a plane descending and spiraling in smaller and smaller circles, as in an accident or feat of expert flying, which if not handled can result in loss of control and a crash. Page 53.

dynamic: active, energetic, effective, forceful, motivating, as opposed to static. From the Greek *dunamikos,* powerful. Page 49.

dynamic(s): the various fields or entities one must cooperate with for optimum survival. The complete description of the dynamics is contained in the article "Ethics, Justice and the Dynamics." Page 31.

E

eclipsed: made less outstanding or important by comparison; surpassed. Page 40.

effect: bring about; accomplish; make happen. Page 80.

efficacy: the capacity for producing a desired result or effect; effectiveness. Page 68.

elders: persons greater than another in age or seniority; also, those senior to others in experience. Page 20.

electroshock: the firing of 180 to 460 volts of electricity through the brain from temple to temple or from the front to the back of one side of the head. It causes a severe convulsion (uncontrollable shaking of the body) or seizure (unconsciousness and inability to control movements of the body) of long duration. Page 68.

emanating: flowing out from; originating or coming from. Page 18.

embezzle: take money or property (that has been given on trust by others) for personal use without their knowledge or permission. Page 20.

emboldened: made bold, courageous or confident. Page 21.

embrace: take in or include, cover; contain; involve. Page 1.

embroiled: involved in conflicts and problems. Page 63.

emotional tone: by *tone* is meant the momentary or continuing emotional state of a person. Emotions such as fear, anger, grief, enthusiasm and others that people experience are shown on a scale, the *Tone Scale,* which indicates how people behave. If people are at a certain level on the Tone Scale, then they behave in a certain way and one can predict how they will behave. Page 31.

endeavor: purposeful or industrious activity. Page 23.

ends: intended results of actions; aims, purposes. Page 35.

enigma: something that is not easily understood; a puzzling or unexplainable situation, event or occurrence. Page 78.

enjoined: directed to do or not do something. Page 88.

enlightened: marked by knowledge or information about something; well-informed. Page 18.

enlivened: made more vigorous, active and interesting. Page 17.

Eoanthropic: of early humans, from the Greek *eo-,* meaning early, and *anthropo,* meaning human. Page 17.

eons: an immeasurably or indefinitely long period of time. Page 60.

epic: of unusually great size or extent. Page 2.

equitable: fair and reasonable in a way that gives equal treatment to everyone. Page 35.

essence, to an: to its basics or fundamentals. Page 87.

estate, grown to man's: reached the age or condition (estate) of being an adult. Page 24.

esteem: favorable opinion or judgment, respect or regard. Page 46.

etiquette: the rules and agreements governing correct or polite behavior in society in general or in a particular social or professional group or situation. Page 33.

evocative: prompting vivid memories or images of things not present. Page 15.

evolutionary psychology: a theory of psychology that focuses on data from the field of biology, attempting to show how evolution shapes behavior, learning, perception, emotion and the like. Page 86.

"Excalibur": a philosophic manuscript written by L. Ron Hubbard in 1938. Although unpublished as such, the body of information it contained has since been released in various Dianetics and Scientology materials. (*Excalibur* was the name of the magic sword of King Arthur, legendary British hero, said to have ruled in the fifth or sixth century A.D.) Page 8.

exculpation: clearing from a charge of guilt or fault; freeing from blame. Page 45.

exile: the act of forcing someone to give up membership in or leave a group, country, etc., usually as a punishment. Page 46.

expense account: the record of an employee's expenses during a particular period. *Pad an expense account* means cheat one's employer by adding false items to an expense account. Page 3.

extenuation: the lessening of blame or punishment. Page 46.

extortion: the obtaining of money from someone by using force, threats or other unfair or illegal methods. Page 71.

extrapolating: using known facts as the starting point from which to draw conclusions about something unknown. Page 8.

eyes at, makes: looks at (someone) flirtatiously. Page 20.

F

fabric: the essential structure of anything; framework. Page 69.

face of it, on the: from appearances alone; apparently; seemingly. Page 18.

fait accompli: a thing already done or made; French phrase meaning an accomplished fact. Page 18.

faith, breaks: violates one's promise or word; acts as a traitor. *Break* means to transgress or violate by disregarding or failing to observe (something); to fail to keep one's word or pledge. *Faith* means a verbal promise, vow or pledge; the duty of fulfilling an obligation. Page 57.

fallacy: a false or mistaken idea; error. Page 18.

fallen: having lost status or moral reputation. Page 99.

fall flat: be completely unsuccessful. Page 103.

fanfare: a noisy or showy display, from the use in music of a *fanfare,* a short, loud dramatic series of notes played on trumpets, as in marking the start of an event, the entrance of someone important or the like. Page 71.

Fascism: a governmental system, led by a dictator having complete power, that forcibly suppresses opposition and criticism and regiments all industry, commerce, etc. Page 30.

fast lane: any scene, activity or pursuit that is exciting, high-pressured, competitive, swift-moving and sometimes dangerous. Literally, the *fast lane* is the lane of a multilane roadway that is used by fast-moving vehicles, as when passing slower traffic. Page 68.

felon: a criminal; a person guilty of a felony. Page 18.

felony: a serious offense, as murder, burglary or the like. Felonies are often classified as punishable by imprisonment for more than a year. Page 45.

fender: a metal or plastic enclosure over the wheels of an automobile or other vehicle to protect against splashing mud, etc. Page 20.

Filipino: a native or inhabitant of the Philippine Islands. Page 37.

filling station: a place that sells gasoline, oil, etc., for motor vehicles. Page 21.

fire trail: a trail or road built in an area, such as a remote part of a forest, to allow access for fire prevention, firefighting or the like. Page 7.

fit: of a suitable or acceptable quality or type, as in *"determine who was 'fit and proper' to serve."* Page 12.

fit, see: consider it right or acceptable to do something; decide or choose to do something. Page 76.

flare up, light begins to: things become clear or are revealed with a sudden intensity. Page 18.

flesh house: the body. Page 20.

flophouse: a cheap hotel or rooming house; from *flop,* lie down, sleep. Page 13.

fobbed off: cheated (someone) by substituting something worthless. Page 3.

folded up: broke down; collapsed; failed. Page 54.

Folsom Prison: a California state prison built in 1880. It is located in the town of Folsom in north central California. Page 109.

footnote: a comment or remark added to a main statement. Page 68.

formula: an exact sequence of steps which one can use to move from the current condition to another, higher and more survival condition. *See also* **condition.** Page 1.

foster: promote or encourage, as in terms of growth, development or the like. Page 18.

fraternity: an ironic reference to a social society for men, such as those who are students at a college or university. Page 16.

***Freedom* magazine:** a magazine published by the Church of Scientology since 1968 that is renowned for its exposure of human rights abuses and investigative journalism. *Freedom* has broken important stories on the forced drugging of schoolchildren, government chemical and biological warfare experimentation and psychiatric brutalities. Page 40.

"free" world: an ironic reference to the *free world,* the nations of the world that function chiefly under democratic systems rather than under some type of dictatorship. Page 42.

French Guiana: a former French colony, now a region administered by France, located on the northeast coast of South America. It became known for its penal colony, established in the mid-1800s, which consisted of several islands and certain parts of the mainland, collectively known as Devil's Island. More than seventy thousand convicts, including political prisoners, habitual criminals and felons, were deported from France to the penal colony between 1852 and the late 1930s. The penal colony was noted for its dreadful conditions, harsh punishment and the undernourishment of those assigned to hard labor. Due to many deaths from the unhealthy climate and few escapes, Devil's Island in French Guiana became known as a place from which no one returned. The French government ceased sending prisoners to the penal colony in 1938 and it was closed in the mid-1900s. Page 23.

freshman: a student in the first year of college in the United States. Page 21.

Freudian: typical of the theories and practices of Sigmund Freud (1856–1939), Austrian founder of psychoanalysis who emphasized that unconscious memories of a sexual nature control a person's behavior. Page 68.

front: an appearance, usually assumed or pretended, of social standing, wealth, etc. From the specialized meaning of *front,* face or expression of the face, indicating state of mind. Page 21.

fronts: areas in which something is happening with regard to a particular field of activity. Page 86.

fruition: attainment of something desired or worked for; accomplishment. Page 107.

fruits: the benefits or advantages of an activity. Page 57.

functionally illiterate: in a condition whereby one's reading and writing abilities are not adequately developed, thus making it difficult or impossible to carry out the everyday activities that require these skills. Page 16.

G

gagging: that would make someone *gag,* nearly choke or vomit, as from revulsion to a food or smell or, used figuratively, in response to events or occurrences that one encounters. Page 20.

gauge: estimate or judge. Page 89.

gavel: a small hammer used by a judge, usually to signal for attention or order. Page 35.

Gaza Strip: a region in the Middle East, lying between Israel and Egypt, an area that has been the subject of dispute for many years. Israel captured the region from Egypt in 1967. Then, in the 1990s, the Gaza Strip came under Palestinian administration. Page 106.

genetic code: the arrangement of genes (basic parts of cells capable of transmitting instructions from one generation to the next) that controls the development of characteristics and qualities in a living thing. Page 67.

genocide: the deliberate killing of a very large number of people from a particular ethnic group or nation. Page 47.

genus: origin. From the Latin *genus,* meaning origin, birth or race. Page 79.

Georgia: a state in the southeastern United States, on the Atlantic Ocean. Page 15.

getaway: an act of leaving a place, especially a quick exit made by somebody who has just committed a crime. Page 20.

Glendale, California: a city in Los Angeles County, southwestern California. Glendale is a residential suburb of Los Angeles. Page 100.

godsend: an unexpected thing or event that is particularly welcome and timely, as if sent by God. Page 104.

Golden Rule: a rule of ethical conduct given in the nonreligious moral code *The Way to Happiness* as *"Try not to do things to others that you would not like them to do to you."* Page 113.

Gómez: Juan Vicente Gómez (1857–1935), Venezuelan dictator, who ruled the country from 1908 until his death in 1935. He discovered the contagion point of leprosy in the country was the beggars, so he had them rounded up and put on two large riverboats that were blown up after launching out into the water. Page 30.

gospel: something, such as an idea or a principle, to be accepted as unquestionably true. Page 86.

grab bag: a collection of things from which one may take whatever he can grab or take possession of. Used figuratively. Page 68.

grass-roots: of, concerning or originating with the common or ordinary people, especially as contrasted with the leaders. Page 103.

graven image(s): an idol carved from stone or wood. *Graven* means carved. Page 87.

grips with, come to: begin to understand and deal with directly or firmly. *Grip* means the grasping of something tightly and in this sense refers to a mental or intellectual hold on something. Page 67.

Group Processing: processing given by a single auditor to a group of individuals gathered in one room. An auditor is a Dianetics or Scientology practitioner. The word *auditor* means one who listens; a listener. *See also* **process(ing).** Page 80.

grown to man's estate: reached the age or condition (estate) of being an adult. Page 24.

guinea pig: somebody or something used as the subject of an experiment or used for any kind of test or trial. A *guinea pig* is a plump, short-eared, furry domesticated animal, native to South America, widely kept as a pet and used as a subject in scientific experiments. Page 68.

gypped: cheated, tricked or swindled. Page 20.

H

habeas corpus: a formal document requiring a person to be brought before a judge or court, especially for investigation of a restraint of the person's liberty, used as a protection against illegal imprisonment. Page 45.

hailed: praised or approved with enthusiasm. Page 111.

hammock(s): a hanging bed, consisting of a length of netting or canvas, etc., suspended by ropes at both ends and used as a bed, especially by sailors on board ships. Page 10.

Hammurabi: (?–1750 B.C.) king of Babylonia (1792–1750 B.C.) who expanded his kingdom into the first great Babylonian empire. He also assembled one of the earliest written collections of laws, known as the Code of Hammurabi. Page 34.

hand in hand: in the manner of things that are inseparably interrelated; in union. Page 54.

haphazard: based on random ideas or guesses rather than on carefully considered judgment or firm knowledge. Page 20.

hardened: firmly established or unlikely to change. Page 11.

harder time, serve even: be in prison for a longer period than the last. Page 16.

hard labor: heavy manual work imposed upon criminals in addition to imprisonment. Page 37.

hardy: capable of enduring difficult conditions; sturdy and of good health. Page 11.

Harlingen, Texas: a city and port in southern Texas near the border of Mexico. It is named for *Harlingen,* a city in the northern Netherlands. Page 104.

hatchet: a small, short-handled instrument with a blade on one side of its head and the form of a hammer on the opposite side. It is made to be used with one hand to chop, split, trim, etc. Page 20.

hazily: in a manner that shows a lack of understanding or knowledge; in a confused or vague way. Page 20.

heads ready for the basket: a reference to the executions that occurred during the French Revolution (1789–1799), when thousands of people were beheaded under the guillotine, with a basket made ready to receive the severed heads. Page 39.

heartening: giving courage or confidence. Page 76.

heart-to-heart: a term used to describe a conversation, discussion, etc., of real frankness and sincerity. Page 13.

hereafter: a life or existence after death; the future beyond mortal existence. Page 86.

heredity theory: the theory that criminal tendencies are due to *heredity,* the passing on of physical or mental characteristics from one generation to another through *genes,* the basic physical units of heredity. Page 23.

herein: in this writing, document or the like. Page 34.

hewing: the action of cutting something with hard or rough repeated blows of a heavy cutting instrument, as a large sword, an ax or the like. Page 17.

hierarchy: a controlling group of any kind; a body of persons having top authority, sometimes in a system arranged in rank, grade, class, etc. Page 72.

high: characterized by outstanding, heroic or stirring events or subject matter; intensely moving or exciting. Page 7.

Hitler: Adolf Hitler (1889–1945), German political leader of the twentieth century who dreamed of creating a master race that would rule for a thousand years as the third German Empire. Taking over rule of Germany by force in 1933 as a dictator, he began World War II (1939–1945), subjecting much of Europe to his domination and murdering millions of Jews and others considered "inferior." He committed suicide in 1945 when Germany's defeat was imminent. Page 61.

hoarded: accumulated for preservation, future use, etc., in a hidden or carefully guarded place. Page 18.

hole: a position from which it is difficult to escape; a mess. Page 60.

holy test tube: figuratively, the worship of all things scientific and the negation of the spirit, as forwarded by psychiatry. Literally, *holy* means worthy of or entitled to worship as, or as if, sacred. A *test tube* is a hollow cylinder of thin glass with one end closed, used in chemical and biological experimentation and analysis. Page 87.

home, drive (something): make a point strongly or firmly. *Drive,* in this case, means press or urge onward; bring about by urgency or pressure. *Home* here means to the vital center or seat; to the very heart or root of the matter. Page 9.

honorable: having or showing a sense of right and wrong; characterized by honesty and integrity. Page 15.

'hood, the: a slang term for *the neighborhood.* Page 68.

hooeyology: a coined term meaning the study of nonsense, bunk or worthless ideas and writings. Page 21.

host(s): 1. somebody who presents and interviews guests on a radio or television program. Page 2.
2. a very large number; a great quantity. Page 8.

humility: the quality or condition of being conscious of one's flaws or failures or having a not-too-high opinion or estimate of one's own abilities, skill, importance, etc. Page 24.

Hutu: people who make up most of the population of Rwanda and Burundi, small neighboring countries in east central Africa. Power struggles from 1959 to the 1990s between the Hutu and the rival Tutsi led to a Hutu campaign of genocide against the Tutsi, who then retaliated, resulting in many hundreds of thousands of deaths. Page 111.

I

ideology: the doctrines, opinions or way of thinking of an individual, class, etc.; specifically, the body of ideas on which a particular political, economic or social system is based. Page 41.

idle: lacking any real worth; serving no useful purpose. Page 20.

illicitly: in a way that is *illicit,* forbidden by law, rules or custom. Page 3.

immoral: not moral; not following good practices of behavior; not doing right; lacking any idea of proper conduct. Page 87.

import: the importance or significance of something. Page 7.

impromptu: done without earlier planning or preparation. Page 30.

inarguable: not open to disagreement; certain. Page 85.

inasmuch as: to the extent or degree, as far as. Page 112.

incapacitating: depriving of ability or strength; making incapable or unfit; disabling. Page 46.

incidence: an instance of something happening or the manner in which it happens. Page 79.

incommunicado, held: prevented by force from communicating with other people. Page 18.

incorrigible: that cannot be corrected or reformed, especially due to firmly established habits. Page 33.

inculcated: imparted or fixed firmly by persistent instruction. Page 105.

incurred: brought upon oneself (something unwelcome or unpleasant) as a result of one's actions. Page 78.

indictment: any charge, accusation or serious criticism. Page 8.

indigenous: originating in and characteristic of a particular region or country; native. Page 29.

inextricable: impossible to get free or escape from. Page 33.

infamy: a lasting, widespread and firmly established evil reputation brought about by something criminal, shocking or brutal. Page 30.

infanticide: the practice of killing newborn babies. Page 54.

infinity: a quality or state of unlimited extent of time, space or quantity. Page 51.

infinity symbol (∞): a mathematical symbol that represents infinity. Page 51.

inflammatory: tending to arouse anger, hostility, passion, etc. Page 86.

ingrained: (of a habit or attitude) firmly established. Page 87.

injunction: an earnest warning. Page 88.

inky: like ink in color; dark; black. Page 17.

innate: existing naturally; inborn; that seems to have been in one from birth. Page 30.

inoculation: protection as if by *inoculating,* injecting with a weakened form of a disease to create or increase immunity in the body to the disease. Page 20.

insanity defense: a legal test used by the courts to determine criminal responsibility or lack thereof. The defense of insanity is based on the belief that someone who is unable to control his actions or appreciate the criminality of his actions due to mental illness should not be punished under criminal law. Page 74.

insider dealing: a criminal offense in which a person who works for a company and has confidential information about the finances of the company uses that information to make a profit in the stock market. Page 3.

insidiously: having a gradual, cumulative and usually hidden destructive effect. Page 63.

insofar as: to such an extent; to such a degree. Page 46.

Ivy League: a group of colleges in the northeastern US forming a league for intercollegiate sports, so called from the fact that many of the buildings are traditionally ivy-covered. The term *Ivy League* is often used to describe the fashions, standards, attitudes, etc., associated with the students attending these colleges. Page 16.

J

Jasov: a small town in eastern Slovakia, a country in east central Europe. Page 106.

"job(s)": a criminal act, especially robbery. Page 21.

John Howard Society, The: an organization in Canada with the objective of preventing crime in society by developing alternatives to imprisonment and various reform and education programs to encourage involvement in and responsibility for the justice system. It is named after John Howard (1726–1790), English philanthropist and prison reformer. Page 75.

joining hands: associating in some action or enterprise; entering into alliance for some particular end. From the sense of people grasping or shaking each others' hands as a sign of agreement. Page 79.

Joliet: a city and river port in northeastern Illinois on the Des Plaines River. It is also the site of the Joliet Correctional Center, the oldest of Illinois' four maximum-security facilities. Page 7.

Ju Chia: the Chinese name for what is known in Western languages as *Confucianism,* the school of thought based on the teachings of the philosopher Confucius (551–479? B.C.). Confucianism has been a dominant influence in Chinese jurisprudence and education for many centuries. In its strictest form, which was upheld particularly by emperors from the 1600s on, Confucianism became a political tool used for control of the population. It stressed that people must remain in their various classes (rulers, scholars, workers, etc.) so that society could be properly managed. Page 30.

judiciary: the system of courts of law for the administration of justice. Page 41.

Judiciary Dianetics: Judiciary Dianetics covers the field of adjudication within the society and among the societies of Man. Of necessity, it embraces jurisprudence (the science or philosophy of law) and its codes and establishes precision definitions and equations for the establishment of equity (fairness). It is the science of judgment. Page 76.

juice: an informal term for electricity or electric power. Page 9.

jurisprudence: the science or philosophy of law; the systematic knowledge of the laws, customs and rights of men in a state or community necessary for the due administration of justice. Page 41.

K

kindly: agreeable; pleasant. Page 23.

L

LAPD: an abbreviation for *Los Angeles Police Department,* the police force of the city of Los Angeles. Page 12.

large, at: as a whole; in general. Page 80.

latchkey: a key used to draw back or unfasten the latch or other lock of a door. Used figuratively. Page 15.

lay: impose something as a burden, penalty or punishment. Page 42.

Leavenworth: a US military base and site of a federal prison. Leavenworth is a city located in the state of Kansas. Page 23.

lest: with the intention of preventing; avoid the risk of. Page 31.

leveled: aimed or directed at or toward. Page 29.

libel: any false or damaging written statement about somebody. Page 42.

Liberalism: a belief or political ideology advocating tolerance and gradual reform in moral, religious or political matters. Liberalism rejects authoritarian government and defends freedom of speech, association and religion. Page 30.

license: 1. a document that gives official permission to a specific person or group to engage in some occupation, do something or own something. Page 12.

2. abusive disregard for what is considered right, proper, etc.; excessive liberty. Page 59.

liquidation: the doing away with or killing of unwanted persons. Page 86.

little people: people who are typical in having a small or average income and minimal power and influence; the common people, especially workers. Page 37.

lofty: having little practical application or value. Page 18.

logical: of or having to do with *logic,* a gradient scale of association of facts of greater or lesser similarity made to resolve some problem of the past, present or future, but mainly to resolve and predict the future. Logic is the combination of factors into an answer. Page 51.

long mile: used to imply a great distance or interval. Page 81.

lynched: put to death, especially by hanging, by mob action and without legal authority. Page 42.

lynchpin: something that holds together the various elements of a complicated structure. Page 35.

M

machinations: secret, cunning or complicated plans or schemes designed to achieve a particular end. Page 35.

magistrate: a public official entrusted with administration of the law, having the power to try minor criminal cases and to conduct preliminary examinations of persons charged with serious crimes. Page 45.

magnetic tape recording: a recording made, as of a person's voice, and later played back to a group of people. *Magnetic tape* is a thin ribbon of material, usually plastic, coated with a substance containing magnetic iron particles and used to record sounds, as in audiocassettes. These particles are bound to the tape with a chemical. Page 80.

Maine: the northernmost state on the east coast of the United States. Page 10.

main, in the: for the most part; mainly. Page 103.

maladjusted: badly or unsatisfactorily adjusted, especially in relationship to one's social circumstances, environment, etc.; unable to cope with the stresses of everyday life. *Adjusted* in this sense means able to deal with and handle the mental and physical factors in one's life with regard to one's own needs and the needs of others. Page 71.

malefactor: a person who has committed a crime. Page 24.

malfeasance: the carrying out of an act that is legally unjustified, harmful or contrary to law by a public official; wrongdoing. Page 2.

malice: desire to inflict injury, harm or suffering on another, either because of a hostile impulse or out of meanness or hatred. Page 46.

Man-from-mud: of or relating to a theory that Man arose from mud. Per this theory, it is alleged that chemicals formed in mud and, through certain combinations and accidental patterns, a primitive single cell was formed. This primitive cell then collided with other such cells and, through accident, formed a more complex structure of single cells that made itself into a unit organism. Supposedly, from this combination of cells, Man was eventually formed. Page 86.

Manhattan, lower: the southern (lower) part of Manhattan, which is one of the five sections that make up New York City and the main economic center of the city. Page 2.

man, to a: with no one as an exception; everyone. Page 23.

Marine Corps: a branch of the United States armed forces trained for land, sea and air combat, typically landing near a battle zone either from the air or from a ship. Page 23.

marksmen: people who are able or trained to shoot accurately at a target, especially with a firearm. Page 59.

materialism: in philosophy, the theory that physical matter is the only reality and that everything, including thought, feeling, mind and will, can be explained in terms of matter and physical phenomena. Page 88.

mayhem: unrestrained destruction; infliction of violent injury upon a person or thing. Page 2.

measure of, a: a certain amount or degree of. Page 9.

MEST: a compound word made up of the first letters of *Matter, Energy, Space* and *Time*. A coined word for the physical universe. Page 50.

metamorphosis: a transformation; a change of form, shape, structure, substance. Page 21.

metaphor: a word or phrase that ordinarily designates one thing used to designate another so as to make a comparison, as in "a sea of troubles" or "All the world's a stage." Page 103.

meted: dealt out. Page 21.

Metropolitan Detective Agency: a California-based detective agency founded in 1936 that provided a variety of services, including missing-person searches, factory protection and patrols. Page 12.

Miami: a city, seaport and tourist resort located on the Atlantic Ocean in southern Florida, a state in the southeastern United States. Page 3.

might: the power, force, authority or collective resources held and used by a group or government. Page 88.

mile, long: used to imply a great distance or interval. Page 81.

military commission: a group of persons in the armed forces who are authoritatively charged with particular functions. Page 30.

mind enough, with: with sufficient reason, sanity or ability. Page 8.

mirage: something that falsely appears to be real. Literally, a mirage is an optical illusion of a sheet of water appearing in the desert or on a hot road, caused by light being distorted by alternate layers of hot and cool air. Page 20.

misdemeanor: a minor criminal offense. Page 45.

misguided: guided in the wrong direction or misled in action or thought; hence, having a wrong purpose or intention, erring in thought or action. Page 62.

mollified: calmed or soothed. Page 13.

monolithic: characterized by massiveness, total uniformity, rigidity, etc. Page 2.

Montana: a state in the western United States, bordering with Canada on the north. The western part of the state is mountainous and the eastern portion is a gently rolling landscape with grazing cattle and sheep. L. Ron Hubbard lived in Montana as a young boy. Page 7.

moral code: an agreed-upon code of right and wrong conduct. Page 1.

Mosaic Code: the law that, according to the Old Testament, God gave to the Israelites through Moses. The Mosaic law begins with the Ten Commandments and includes the many rules of religious observance given in the first five books of the Old Testament. In Judaism, these books are called the Torah, or "the Law." Page 87.

mounted: prepared and launched, as an attack or a campaign. Page 87.

N

Nagasaki: a city and port in southern Japan, on which the United States dropped the second atomic bomb used in warfare, on 9 August 1945, during World War II (1939–1945). It killed forty thousand people and injured as many. Page 30.

Napoleon: Napoleon Bonaparte (1769–1821), French military leader. He rose to power in France by military force, declared himself emperor and conducted campaigns of conquest across Europe. A defeat in 1814 led to his exile to a small island off the northwestern coast of Italy. After a brief return to power and final defeat in 1815, he was imprisoned on the tiny, mountainous island of St. Helena, in the South Atlantic Ocean. Page 61.

"National" Mental Health groups: a reference to *National Mental Health Associations,* private, profit-making organizations established in various countries. They are under the World Federation for Mental Health. They work to get laws passed that will enable psychs to pick up people freely and put them into mental hospitals. By using the word *national* in their name, these groups pretend that they are part of a government, but they are not. Page 72.

Native American: a member of any of the groups of people regarded as originating in North America before the arrival of the first Europeans. Page 13.

Naval School of Military Government: a school of military government established at Princeton University, Princeton, New Jersey, in October 1944. The purpose was to train navy officers so as to provide needed personnel for projected military government activities as well as for specialized civilian duties. Page 29.

Nazis: members of the National Socialist German Workers' Party, which in 1933, under Adolf Hitler, seized political control of the country, suppressing all opposition and establishing a dictatorship over all activities of the people. It promoted and enforced the belief that the German people were superior and that the Jews were inferior (and thus were to be eliminated). The party was officially abolished in 1945 at the conclusion of World War II (1939–1945). *Nazi* is from the first part of the German word for the name of the party, *Nationalsozialist,* which is pronounced *nazi* in German. Page 41.

neural: of or pertaining to a nerve or the nervous system. Page 69.

New Orleans: a city and seaport in southeastern Louisiana, a state in the southern United States. Page 3.

New Social Darwinism: *Social Darwinism* was a nineteenth-century theory that human societies and races follow the same biological laws of natural selection as plants and animals. *Natural selection* is the process, according to English biologist Charles Darwin (1809–1882), whereby organisms better adapted to their environment tend to survive and produce more offspring. In the 1960s and 1970s, *New Social Darwinism* picked up the earlier theory, attempting to show that intelligence and behavior are determined by genetics rather than by cultural influences, thus indicating that some societies or races are more advanced than others because their members are biologically superior. Page 86.

nomadic: characteristic of or relating to *nomads,* those who are part of a group that moves from place to place seasonally in search of pasture for their herds or food and water. Page 87.

non-survival: from *non,* implying negation or absence of, and *survival.* Hence non-survival is a negation or absence of *survival,* the act of remaining alive, of continuing to exist, of being alive. Page 53.

not for nothing: for a very good reason. Page 111.

notwithstanding: in spite of; regardless of. Page 14.

oblivion: destruction or extinction. Also, a state of complete forgetfulness or unawareness. Page 85.

obscene: disgusting and morally offensive, especially because of showing total disregard for other people. Page 86.

obtuse: hard to understand; so scholarly as to be unclear. Page 2.

occasioned: brought about; caused. Page 17.

occupation forces: the troops assigned to maintain control of a newly conquered region until the conclusion of hostilities or establishment of a settled government. Page 29.

occupied territories: regions that are held by occupation forces. *See also* **occupation forces.** Page 29.

odious: arousing dislike or intense displeasure; detestable. Page 41.

officialdom: officials as a class or as a body, especially when viewed as inefficient or unhelpful. Page 10.

oil crisis: a shortage of oil occurring in the United States and certain European countries beginning in the early 1970s. The shortage was caused mainly by restrictions placed on oil trade by the Organization of Petroleum Exporting Countries (OPEC), which regulated the amount of oil produced by its member countries and set the prices for its export. The restrictions were intended to punish the United States and some of its allies for supporting Israel in its 1973 conflict with the Arab states. The situation caused widespread panic, severe shortages of gasoline and extremely inflated prices. The crisis continued at varying levels through the 1970s and by 1980 oil prices were ten times those of 1973. Page 56.

on par with: equal to or at the same level as; generally having the same status. Page 110.

oratory: pompous, boring or inappropriately long speech. Page 17.

order of the day: the characteristic or dominant custom, feature or activity of a particular time. Page 40.

organism: any living thing. Page 52.

Orient: the countries of eastern Asia, especially China, Japan and their neighbors. Page 30.

ostracized: excluded, by general consent, from society, friendship, conversation, privileges, etc. Page 33.

outmoded: not acceptable by present standards; obsolete. Page 59.

overlord(s): a person of great influence, authority, power or the like. Page 23.

oxymoron: a figure of speech by which a word, phrase or expression produces a seemingly self-contradictory effect. Page 35.

P

packing weapons: carrying weapons, such as guns, knives or the like. Page 3.

palpable: easily perceptible by the mind or one of the senses, as to be almost able to be felt physically. Page 33.

paltry: (of a sum of money) very small and of little or no value; insignificant. Page 110.

paradigm: an example serving as a model; pattern. Page 68.

pardon: the official release from any, or any further, punishment of somebody who has committed a crime or wrongdoing; the action of forgiving or being forgiven for an error or offense. Page 35.

park spooners: a slang term for those who sentimentally kiss and caress in a park. Page 21.

parliamentary: of or relating to *parliaments,* official or formal conferences or councils, usually concerned with government or public affairs, such as proposing to correct or create new laws. Page 46.

parole board: a group of persons having the authority to grant a prisoner an early release from prison on parole. *Parole* means a release of a prisoner either temporarily for a special purpose or permanently before the completion of a jail sentence, on the promise of good behavior. Page 23.

Parris Island: a United States Marine Corps recruit and training station in southeast South Carolina. Parris Island consists of several islands extending over 7,000 acres, with only 3,200 of these habitable. Spending the majority of their time training in the uninhabitable sections of the land, Marine Corps recruits pass initiation into the world of the US Marines. Parris's motto is "We don't train recruits...we make Marines." Page 23.

part and parcel: an indivisible element in something. Page 57.

par with, on: equal to or at the same level as; generally having the same status. Page 110.

passion: as used in certain laws, a reference to any intense emotion, such as rage, anger, hatred, resentment or terror, that renders the mind incapable of calm consideration. Page 46.

patterns: combinations of qualities, acts, tendencies, etc., forming consistent or characteristic arrangements. Page 77.

Pavlov: Ivan Petrovich Pavlov (1849–1936), Russian physiologist, noted for his dog experiments. Pavlov presented food to a dog while he sounded a bell. After repeating this procedure several times, the dog (in anticipation) would salivate at the sound of the bell, whether or not food was presented. Pavlov concluded that all acquired habits, even the higher mental activity of Man, depended on conditioning. Page 67.

peddle: sell something illegal, especially drugs. Page 59.

Peking: former name of Beijing, the capital of China. Page 30.

pen: a shortened form of *penitentiary*, a prison maintained in the United States by a state or federal government for serious offenders. Page 23.

penal: of, relating to or involving punishment, as for crimes or offenses. Page 34.

Penal Code: a body of laws concerned with various crimes or offenses and their legal penalties. Page 44.

penitentiary: a prison maintained in the United States by a state or the federal government for serious offenders. Page 7.

per capita: per person or unit of population. Page 12.

perpetrated: committed or performed. Page 59.

persecution: also called *persecution complex,* the feeling of being *persecuted,* subjected to cruel or unfair treatment, especially without basis in reality. Page 79.

persuasion: a form or system of religious or other beliefs, ideas, views, opinions or the like. Page 46.

petty offenders: individuals who break certain lesser laws, usually city laws, and are arrested on such charges as disturbing the peace, trespassing, being a public nuisance and so on. Page 14.

piety: enthusiastic devotion to religious duties and worship; reverence and obedience to God. Page 87.

pinnacle: the highest or topmost point or level of something. Page 2.

pivotal: of vital or critical importance. Page 14.

plane: a level of existence or thought. Page 52.

plea bargaining: an agreement between a prosecutor and a defendant whereby the defendant is allowed to plead guilty to a lesser charge rather than risk conviction for a graver crime to avoid a long trial or to win the defendant's cooperation as a witness. Page 35.

pointed: serving to make something quite obvious. Page 13.

point of fact, in: with regard to matters of fact. Page 33.

polysyllabic: consisting of several, especially four or more, syllables (words or parts of words pronounced with a single, uninterrupted sounding of the voice), such large words sometimes being employed by those who act very learned and serious. Page 18.

pompous: characterized by an exaggerated display of self-importance or dignity. Page 18.

pond scum: a layer of green freshwater algae on the surface of stagnant water. *Algae* are any of several divisions of simple organisms having no true root, stem or leaf. They are found in water or damp places. Most algae use the energy of sunlight to make their own food. Page 87.

Portland: the largest city and a major center of industry and trade in Oregon, a state in the northwestern United States. Page 9.

Port Orchard: a resort and fishing community located in western Washington State on *Puget Sound,* a long, narrow bay of the Pacific Ocean on the northwestern coast of the United States. Page 37.

Portsmouth Naval Prison: a naval prison that is part of the Portsmouth Naval Shipyard, a naval shipyard built in the 1790s and located in Kittery, Maine. Kittery is situated across the Piscataqua River from Portsmouth, New Hampshire. Both Portsmouth and Kittery were founded in 1623 and have been important ports for fishing and shipbuilding. Page 10.

post-Biblical: characteristic of the times that are after (post) the time period covered in the Bible. The events described in the Bible correspond to a period from about 1300 B.C. to the second century A.D. Page 87.

posture: a policy, an attitude or an approach toward something, especially as perceived by the public, other nations, etc. Page 74.

power(s): a person, organization or nation having great influence, authority or control over others. Page 43.

practice license: to engage in abusive disregard for what is considered right, proper, etc.; to take excessive liberty. Page 59.

precedent(s): a previous instance or case that is, or may be, taken as an example or rule for subsequent cases or by which some similar act or circumstance may be supported or justified. Page 32.

precepts: rules, instructions or principles that guide somebody's actions, especially ones that guide moral behavior. Page 88.

precipitated: brought about, often quickly, suddenly or unexpectedly; caused. Page 11.

preclude: prevent the occurrence of or make it impossible for someone to do something. Page 29.

predicated (on): (said of a statement or action) based or established on. Page 35.

premise(s): something presumed to be true and used as a basis for developing an idea. Page 14.

pressure group(s): a group that tries to get laws passed that favor its own interests (as by promoting, urging and otherwise working to influence legislators). Page 41.

prey: a person or thing that is the intended target of someone or something. Page 78.

primordial: first or earliest formed; primitive; related to the earliest stages of formation (of something). Page 87.

Princeton (University): a leading United States university located in Princeton, New Jersey (a state in the eastern United States). In the 1940s, it housed a school of government to train navy and army officers so as to provide needed personnel for projected military government activities. Page 29.

prison colony: a place of confinement and punishment for a group of criminals. Since the 1700s, some European countries sent many criminals to their colonies in North America and Australia

(Great Britain) and South America (France). In some prison colonies, prisoners were subjected to harsh living conditions and heavy work. Page 23.

process(ing): a *process* is a systematic and technically exact series of steps, actions or changes to bring about a specific and definite result. In Scientology, a *process* is a precise series of techniques or exercises applied by a practitioner to help a person find out more about himself and his life and to improve his condition. The action of applying a process or processes is called *processing*. Page 80.

proliferation: a rapid (and often excessive) spread or increase of something. Page 86.

propensity: a natural inclination or tendency. Page 67.

pro-survival: from *pro,* in favor of, and *survival.* Hence *pro-survival* is something in favor of or in support of *survival,* the act of remaining alive, of continuing to exist, of being alive. Page 59.

provisions: arrangements for future eventualities or requirements. Page 33.

provost court: a military court convened in occupied territory under military government, usually composed of one officer and empowered to try military personnel and civilians for minor offenses. Page 30.

psychobabble: writing or talk that, using the language and concepts of psychology or psychiatry, is trite, superficial and deliberately confusing. Page 68.

psychopath(s): a person whose behavior is largely anti-social and without morals, who is characterized by irresponsibility, lack of remorse or shame, criminal behavior and other serious personality defects, generally without psychotic attacks or symptoms. Page 75.

psychosomatic: *psycho* refers to mind and *somatic* refers to body; the term *psychosomatic* means the mind making the body ill or illnesses which have been created physically within the body by the mind. A description of the cause and source of psychosomatic ills is contained in *Dianetics: The Modern Science of Mental Health*. Page 11.

psychosurgical: of or having to do with *psychosurgery,* the use of brain surgery as a supposed treatment for mental disorders. Page 68.

psychotropic: affecting mental activity, behavior or perception. Page 47.

public treasury: the public funds or revenues of a government or the place where they are received, kept, disbursed and recorded. Page 18.

purveyance: the act or process of *purveying,* obtaining or supplying something for use. Page 47.

push-button: characterized by, or as if by, the use of a *push button,* a device that, when depressed, closes or opens an electric circuit; operating in an automatic manner. Page 71.

Q

quarter: a particular but unspecified person, group, area or place. Page 1.

quipped: made a clever or witty comment. Page 10.

R

ranger: an officer whose job is to patrol and guard a forest. Page 7.

rank and file: the members of a group or organization apart from its leaders or officers. Page 24.

ransom: a sum of money demanded or paid for the release of somebody who is being held prisoner. Page 47.

rapacity: the condition of being excessively greedy, especially for money, and willing to use whatever means to obtain what is desired. Page 2.

rap sheet: a slang term for a record kept by law enforcement authorities of a person's arrests and convictions. Page 34.

rationality: power to draw conclusions that enable one to understand the world about him and relate such knowledge to the attainment of personal and common ends; power to reason or being in accordance with what reason dictates as being right, wise, sensible, etc. Page 1.

raw: brutal, harsh. Page 37.

reactively: irrationally; in a manner that shows one is affected by the *reactive mind,* that portion of a person's mind which works on a totally stimulus-response basis (given a certain stimulus it gives a certain response), which is not under his volitional control, and which exerts force and the power of command over his awareness, purposes, thoughts, body and actions. Page 60.

reason: sound judgment; good sense, as in *"this grand view of ethics as reason itself."* Page 32.

reasonable: using or showing reason or sound judgment; sensible. Page 46.

recalcitrant: resisting authority or control; not obedient or compliant. Page 9.

recidivism: repeated or habitual relapse into criminal habits. Page 16.

recoil: draw back; jump or shrink back, as in alarm, horror or disgust. Page 80.

recourse: the means by which one can obtain help or a solution to a problem. Page 42.

redress: the correcting of a wrong situation that a person has experienced. Page 35.

red revolution: a forceful revolution, intending sweeping social or political reform. *Red* means inciting or endorsing sweeping social or political reform, especially by the use of force; from the flag used by revolutionaries. A *revolution* is an overthrow or rejection and thorough replacement of an established government or political system by the people governed. Page 37.

referendum: the submission of a law, proposed or already in effect, to a direct vote of the people. Page 3.

reflective: that clearly shows; indicative. Page 87.

reform school: an institution to which young offenders convicted of lesser crimes are sent for training and discipline intended to reform rather than punish them. Page 21.

relief: goods or money given by a government agency to people because of need or poverty. Page 24.

remorse: deep and painful regret for wrongdoing. Page 111.

render: make, cause to be or become of a certain nature, quality, etc. Page 34.

reprehensible: deserving strong disapproval or criticism. Page 32.

repress: keep under control; restrain. Page 79.

repute: the opinion generally held of someone or something; the state of being generally regarded in a particular way. Page 45.

resounding: 1. very great; impressively complete. Page 1.

2. making a loud, long or reverberating sound. Page 35.

retention: the action of *retaining,* paying or keeping in one's service to do work. Page 46.

revolving door: any system in which people frequently enter and leave, such as a criminal-justice system that puts offenders in prison, releases them and then puts them back in prison. From the literal idea of a *revolving door,* a type of door often used in large buildings, consisting of four panels that intersect at right angles and turn on a central pivot so that the door continues rotating. Page 16.

rim, on the: at the very edge of something, especially, at a crucial or critical point of a situation or state beyond which success or catastrophe occurs. Page 2.

ripe: ready to do, receive or undergo something; fully prepared, likened to fruit that is fully developed and ready to be picked and eaten. Page 3.

Ripley: Robert Ripley (1890–1949), American cartoonist and artist who became famous for his cartoon *Believe It or Not,* which featured oddities and strange facts and occurrences from around the world. Page 18.

ritual(s): 1. a practice or pattern of behavior regularly performed in a set manner; the performance of formal acts. Page 35.

2. a set of fixed actions and sometimes words performed regularly, especially as part of a religious ceremony or social custom. Page 67.

rogue: characteristic of an animal driven away or living apart from others of its kind and having vicious, destructive tendencies. Page 68.

Roma: also called *Gypsies,* people originally from India who adopted a wandering lifestyle and migrated west over the centuries. Many Roma live in eastern and central Europe. Page 106.

romantic novels: novels representing heroic or marvelous deeds, romantic exploits, usually in a historical or imaginary setting. Page 57.

Rome: the city (and later, the empire) of ancient Rome, which at its peak included western and southern Europe, Britain, North Africa and the lands of the eastern Mediterranean Sea and which lasted from the 500s B.C. into the A.D. 400s. The last years of the empire (fourth century and part of the fifth century) were marked by steady decline: economic disintegration, weak emperors, invading tribes and a central government providing few services and little protection while demanding more taxes. Page 85.

Royal Commission of Canada: a group of persons authoritatively charged by the government of Canada to inquire into and establish recommendations regarding a particular matter. Page 74.

rubber stamp: an approval from an official of a government that is given automatically, without reviewing, thinking or questioning. Page 12.

ruling passion: a chief or predominating object of intense interest in a particular subject or activity. Page 54.

rusty wings, vulture's: refers to the rust-colored feathers on the broad wings of the *vulture,* the name of various large birds of prey that feed chiefly on dead and decaying animal flesh. Most are bare of feathers on the head and neck, have a slightly hooked beak and can have a wingspan of up to 10½ feet (3.2 meters). Page 21.

S

Sabbath: Saturday, the seventh day of the week, observed by Jews as a day of worship and of rest from work. This observance is a reminder of the Biblical story of the Creation, in which God created the world in six days and rested on the seventh day. Some Christians also observe Saturday as a holy day, while most observe it on Sunday. The word comes from Hebrew, *shavat,* to rest or cease. Page 87.

salient: that stands out as important; particularly relevant. Page 44.

Savannah: a seaport on the Atlantic coast in Georgia, a southeastern state of the United States. Page 14.

save: with the exception of; except. Page 79.

savor of: seem to have a specified quantity or quality of something; seem to involve. Page 77.

savvy: experienced and well-informed. Page 67.

Scientology: the term Scientology is taken from the Latin *scio,* which means "knowing in the fullest sense of the word," and the Greek word *logos,* meaning "study of." In itself the word means literally "knowing how to know." Scientology is further defined as the study and handling of the spirit in relationship to itself, universes and other life. Page 1.

screw: a slang term for a prison guard. *Screw* was originally slang for a key. One of the most important functions of a prison guard is to see that prisoners are locked up at the appropriate times—and that involves turning the "screw." Hence, the extension of the word to the guards themselves. Page 23.

scrupulously: in a way that is *scrupulous,* extremely honest; doing everything correctly and exactly as it should be done. Page 43.

seamanship: knowledge and skill pertaining to the operation, navigation, management, safety and maintenance of a ship. Page 10.

sea watch: a watch (a period of time into which a day is divided, during which a part of a ship's company remains on duty) aboard a ship at sea. *Standing sea watches* refers to, for example, a period of time during which a sailor would handle an assigned duty, such as monitoring radar, doing lookout, etc. Page 10.

secular: of or pertaining to things that are not regarded as religious or sacred. Page 86.

sedatives: drugs that are primarily used to induce drowsiness and sleep. Sedatives are habit-forming and can cause severe addiction problems. Page 62.

seep: enter or penetrate gradually. Page 69.

see through: perceive and comprehend the true meaning, character, nature of; detect. Page 41.

segregation: the separating of one person, group or thing from others; the dividing of people or things into separate groups kept apart from each other. Page 78.

seizure: the capturing or taking by force of someone or something, often with official or legal authorization. Page 42.

sentence, in a: in a simple, comprehensive statement; briefly. Page 87.

serve even harder time: be in prison for a longer period than the last. Page 16.

service record: the record of a person's employment in a branch of military service. For example, a naval service record contains documents such as birth certificate, school certificates, letters of commendation, enlistment contract, history of assignments, performance record, medical record, rank, etc. Page 10.

1789, another: another *French Revolution,* a revolt in France from 1789 to 1799 that overthrew the royal family and the aristocratic class and system of privileges they enjoyed. The revolution was in part a protest against France's absolute monarchy, its firmly established and unproductive nobility and the consequent lack of freedom for the middle classes. During the revolution, thousands of people were beheaded under the guillotine. Page 39.

Shanghai: a seaport and the largest city in China, located on the eastern coast of the country. Shanghai is a center of industry, trade and finance. Page 30.

sheer: considered or viewed by itself alone, without reference to or including anything else. Page 1.

shortcomings: failures or deficiencies in conduct, condition, thought, ability, etc. Page 51.

side arm: a weapon such as a pistol that is worn at the waist, usually on a belt. Page 13.

sight(s): any of various mechanical or optical viewing devices, as on a firearm, for aiding the eye in aiming. Page 21.

signed on: agreed to do a particular job; started working for. Page 7.

Sing Sing: a famous New York state prison in the village of Ossining, north of New York City, built in the 1820s. Known for its extreme discipline, the prison has also carried out hundreds of death penalties. Page 8.

singular: exceptional; remarkable; especially effective. Page 2.

slander: a false tale or report maliciously uttered with the intent to injure the reputation of another. Page 46.

slates were clean: being given a new start or fresh chance after offenses of the past had been put aside. A *slate* is a thin piece or plate of rock used for writing on with chalk. From the practice in nineteenth-century taverns of recording a customer's debts on a slate with a chalk. Once the debt was paid, the record would be wiped off and the customer had a "clean slate." A person's experiences have often been compared to the writing accumulated on a slate. Page 10.

small-time: having little or no importance or influence. Page 21.

sneering: characterized by the expression of scorn or contempt. Page 103.

snow-eater: a slang term for someone who takes drugs; a cocaine user. Page 21.

social: forming, or having a tendency to form, cooperative and interdependent relationships with one's fellows; relating to or concerned with the welfare of human beings as members of society. Page 11.

social animal: Man conceived of as being an animal who lives in, or is inclined to live in, communities. Page 76.

social structure: the organization of a community of people living in a particular country or region and having shared customs, laws and the like. Page 41.

sociobiologist: a specialist in *sociobiology*, the study of social behavior in animals, with emphasis on the role of behavior in survival and reproduction. Page 86.

sociological: having to do with or pertaining to *sociology*, the science or study of the origin, development, organization and functioning of human society; the science of the fundamental laws of social relations, institutions, etc. Page 2.

sociopathic: of or having to do with a *sociopath*, one whose behavior is largely criminal, anti-social and without morals and who lacks any sense of responsibility, remorse or shame. Page 3.

sorriest: inspiring an extreme degree of sorrow, pity, scorn and ridicule. Page 17.

sound: based on good sense and valid reasoning. Page 76.

South Pacific: region of the Pacific Ocean lying south of the equator, including its islands, many of which saw heavy fighting during World War II (1939–1945). Page 9.

spawned: brought forth; produced. Page 3.

Special Officer: a patrol officer licensed by the police department. Special Officers either remain in a specific area to guard it or patrol a neighborhood on behalf of the local merchants. They are armed, uniformed and generally have the same duties as a regular police officer when on patrol. Page 2.

species: a group or class of animals or plants having certain common and permanent characteristics that clearly distinguish it from other groups and which can breed with one another. Page 56.

spooners, park: a slang term for those who sentimentally kiss and caress in a park. Page 21.

stamped: marked with a distinctive or lasting characteristic. Page 16.

stand: a position or attitude regarding a particular subject. Page 81.

stand for: tolerate or put up with something. Page 42.

starkness: harshness or grimness, as a view, place, etc. Page 79.

static: pertaining to or characterized by a fixed or stationary condition, lacking movement or motion. Page 33.

steam, under one's own: unaided; by one's own efforts; without any help from others. Page 35.

stickup: an armed robbery. Page 21.

stimulus-response: a certain stimulus (something that rouses a person or thing to activity or energy or that produces a reaction in the body) automatically giving a certain response. Page 71.

St. Louis: a city and port in the eastern part of the state of Missouri, on the Mississippi River. Page 3.

strained: (of personal relations, a situation, etc.) subjected to a dangerous degree of tension; forced to a point of threatened disharmony. Page 63.

string to pull: figuratively, a clue or lead to follow; something that one cannot understand and that one inquires into further to try to understand, likened to pulling on a piece of string that is sticking out. Page 86.

subvert: overthrow a condition or order of things, a principle, law, etc.; overturn. Page 46.

suffice (it) to say: used to indicate that one is presenting something in a brief way, without necessarily giving all the details. Page 22.

sullen: dark, unpleasant and depressing. Page 17.

summarily: in a prompt and direct manner; immediately and without delay. Page 106.

summary: 1. immediate; with little discussion, investigation or attention to formalities. Page 10.
2. a concise and comprehensive statement giving the main points or substance of a matter. Page 48.

sundered: broken or split apart; separated. Page 88.

sun, in the: figuratively, free from worry or sorrow; free from darkness. It also refers to a position favorable or advantageous to one's future. Literally, *in the sun* means one can feel the sun's rays, see the sunshine, sunlight, etc. Page 20.

superimposed: imposed or placed on or upon another; laid above or on the top. *Super-* means over, above or on and *impose* means to place on or onto. Page 72.

supermax: describing a prison that is made secure by the most extensive and elaborate security arrangements that are available or in current use. Page 111.

suppress: to squash, to sit on, to make smaller, to refuse to let reach, to make uncertain about his reaching, to render or lessen in any way possible by any means possible to the harm of the individual and for the fancied protection of the suppressor. Page 54.

Supreme Being: God, regarded as the creator and ruler of the universe. Page 49.

Supreme Court: the highest court in the United States. The Supreme Court consists of nine judges appointed by the president who make decisions solely on constitutional matters. Page 88.

survival of the fittest: the theory that there is an operation of natural causes by which the individuals of a species that are best adapted to the environment tend to be preserved and to transmit their characteristics (through reproduction), while those less adapted die out, so that in the course of generations the degree of adaptation to the environment tends progressively to increase. Page 87.

swell: become greater in intensity or amount; expand. Page 37.

T

tabulated: arranged (facts, statistics, etc.) into a table, columns or other systematically organized grouping. Page 18.

talk-radio: of or relating to a radio format featuring talk shows and listener call-ins. Page 2.

Tao: the *Tao Teh King,* the doctrine and philosophy written by Lao-tzu (sixth century B.C.) in verse form. It literally means "the way" and is the foundation of *Taoism,* a Chinese philosophy that advocates a simple life and a policy of noninterference with the natural course of things. Page 30.

Taoism: a Chinese religion and philosophy based on the doctrines of Lao-tzu (sixth century B.C.), one of the great philosophers of China. Taoism advocates a simple life and a policy of noninterference with the natural course of things. *Tao* means literally "the way." Page 30.

Tasmania: a state of southeastern Australia, consisting of the island Tasmania and several smaller islands, lying 150 miles (240 kilometers) south of mainland Australia. In the 1800s the Port Arthur penal settlement was located there, housing up to two thousand prisoners at a time and known for its harsh discipline. Page 23.

technology: the methods of application of an art or science as opposed to mere knowledge of the science or art itself. In Scientology, the term *technology* refers to the methods of application of Scientology principles to improve the functions of the mind and rehabilitate the potentials of the spirit, developed by L. Ron Hubbard. Page 1.

Tel Aviv: a city in west central Israel, on the Mediterranean Sea. Page 103.

telling: revealing; that tells or reveals much. Page 3.

temperate: showing moderation or self-restraint. Page 88.

Ten Commandments: the ten religious laws of God that governed the ancient Hebrews and were later accepted as fundamental principles of the Christian belief. Page 87.

tenement: a run-down and often overcrowded apartment house. Page 56.

term: a limited period for which something lasts or is intended to last. Page 10.

termites: pale-colored, soft-bodied insects that live in colonies and feed on wood. Some are very destructive to wooden structures and trees. Page 86.

test by fire: an introductory or initial experience that is a severe ordeal. Page 23.

Texas: a state in the southwest United States. Page 104.

theorist, legal: one who deals mainly with the philosophy of law in order to arrive at an understanding of the nature of law, principles of right and wrong, legal systems and legal institutions. Page 74.

thereof: of the thing just mentioned; of that. Page 46.

thereto: to that thing just mentioned. Page 45.

Third Reich: a term adopted by Adolf Hitler during the 1920s to describe the thousand-year regime he intended to create in Germany by conquering Europe. *Reich* is a German word meaning state or empire. Page 86.

three score and ten: seventy years, viewed as the average length of time a person is likely to live. A score equals twenty years. Page 20.

time, serve even harder: be in prison for a longer period than the last. Page 16.

tooth and claw: a variation of *tooth and nail,* with the use of one's teeth and nails as weapons, by biting and scratching. Used figuratively in the way of vigorous attack, defense or action generally; vigorously, fiercely, with one's utmost efforts, with all one's might. Page 87.

tossed off: disregarded or thrown aside in an unthinking way. Page 67.

tough case: a person who is rough or violent. Page 21.

tractable: easily managed or controlled. Page 69.

tragedy: a very sad event or situation, especially one involving death or suffering. Page 62.

tranquilizer(s): any of certain drugs given as a supposed calming agent in controlling various emotional conditions. Page 62.

transient: staying in a place for only a short period of time. Page 13.

Tutsi: an African people who live mainly in the central African nations of Burundi and Rwanda. The Tutsi are a minority group, but one that has traditionally held power. Fighting between them and the numerically superior Hutu has led to hundreds of thousands of deaths since the mid-1990s. Page 111.

.22 pistol: a handgun having a barrel with a bore measuring approximately one-quarter of an inch (.22 inch or 5.58 millimeters) in diameter. Page 21.

twinge: a feeling of mental or emotional distress, shame, sorrow or the like. Page 21.

tyrannical: unjustly cruel, harsh or severe; arbitrary or oppressive. Page 20.

U

U-boat: a German submarine, especially one used during World Wars I (1914–1918) and II (1939–1945). From German *U-Boot,* short for *Unterseeboot,* literally, undersea boat. Page 9.

unarguable: not open to argument, dispute or question. Page 88.

uncouth: of strange and unpleasant or distasteful character. Page 20.

underscore: emphasize something, likened to marking with a score (line drawn or scratched) underneath the printed words on a page. Page 7.

undress blues: the everyday uniform of a sailor, consisting of blue trousers and shirt with long sleeves and a broad square collar hanging down in back. Page 10.

unduly: improperly or unjustly. Page 104.

unharness: release (energy, passions or the like) from restraints. Page 78.

unprecedented: never having happened before; having no earlier equivalent. Page 105.

unqualified: complete, total; not modified, limited or restricted. Page 79.

unwittingly: unknowingly; unconsciously; without awareness. Page 32.

urban sprawl: the expansion of a city into areas of countryside that surround it. Page 12.

usher in: precede and introduce; inaugurate. Page 89.

USMC: an abbreviation for the *United States Marine Corps.* Page 23.

usurped: (of a position, standing or the like) taken over wrongfully, as without authority or right. Page 87.

utterances: things expressed, as words, whether written or spoken. Page 46.

V

vacuum for trouble: someone who tends to bring distress, concern, worry or danger upon himself. A *vacuum* is an enclosed space from which the air and particles have been removed. As a result, air outside the space pushes in on the vacuum and tries to fill it. Page 60.

vain, in: in a way that is casual or does not show proper respect. Page 87.

vantage point: a position or location that provides a broad view or perspective of something. Page 32.

vehemence: the quality of being *vehement,* expressing something with conviction or intense feeling. Page 30.

venture: embark upon a daring course of action; dare to go. Page 24.

veritable: possessing all of the distinctive qualities of the person or thing specified. Page 2.

victimize(d): cause to suffer trouble, discomfort, annoyance, irritation, etc.; cause to become a victim (one who suffers from a destructive or injurious action). Page 76.

Vietnam: a tropical country in Southeast Asia, site of a major war from 1954 to 1975 between South Vietnam and Communist-controlled North Vietnam. The United States became involved in the mid-1960s, lending its support to South Vietnam. By the late 1960s, due to the length of the war, high US casualties and US participation in war crimes against the Vietnamese, American involvement became increasingly unpopular in the US and was strongly protested. In 1973, despite continuing hostilities between North and South Vietnam, the US removed all its troops. By 1975, the Communists had overrun South Vietnam and the war was officially ended, leading to the unification of the country (1976) as the Socialist Republic of Vietnam. Page 56.

villainy: evil conduct; extreme wickedness. Page 57.

Vinaya Pitaka: scriptures covering the rules governing the conduct of Buddhist monks and nuns. It consists of more than 225 rules (each accompanied by a story explaining the original reason for it) that are arranged according to the seriousness of the offense resulting from their violation. The name *Vinaya Pitaka* means basket of discipline. Page 32.

vindictive: said or done in revenge; characterized by vengeance. Page 44.

virtue: the worth, advantage or beneficial quality of something. Page 42.

virulent: extremely injurious or deadly. Page 111.

virus: anything that corrupts or poisons the mind; evil or harmful influence. Page 20.

vociferous: characteristic of loud, noisy, repeated expression of opinions, complaints or demands. Page 3.

W

wake of, in the: *wake* is the visible trail (of agitated and disturbed water) left by something, such as a ship, moving through water. Hence a condition left behind someone or something that has passed; following as a consequence. Page 104.

waning: decreasing in strength, power or influence; declining. Page 88.

want of: absence or deficiency of something desirable or requisite; lack. Page 68.

warped: literally, bent or twisted out of shape, especially out of a straight or flat form. Figuratively, *warped* means twisted or distorted from the truth, fact, true meaning, etc. Page 53.

way of, in the: of the nature of, belonging to the class of; as regards to (something). Page 3.

way out, on the: going down in status or condition; dying. Page 53.

wayward: turned or turning away from what is right or proper. Page 99.

weed(s): marijuana, specifically a marijuana cigarette for smoking as a drug. Page 47.

West Bank: an area in the Middle East between the western bank of the Jordan River and the eastern frontier of Israel. Occupied by Israel in 1967, the West Bank has a large Palestinian majority. During the 1990s, many parts of the West Bank were transferred to Palestinian administration. Page 106.

Western: of or pertaining to the countries and people of Europe and the Americas. Page 2.

western(s): a story having to do with the American West during the 1800s, a period of development and expansion of the frontier. Page 7.

wherewithal: the necessary means, especially financial ones, required for a purpose. Page 49.

white-collar crime: any of various crimes, such as stealing funds, equipment, etc., of a business, committed by business or professional people while working at their occupations. *White-collar* means pertaining to the ranks of office and professional workers whose jobs generally do not involve manual labor or the wearing of a uniform or work clothes. Page 3.

will: wish, want or preference involving deliberate intention, choice or determination. Page 18.

Wilson, Edward O.: Edward Osborne Wilson (1929–), American biologist, known for research on ants, to which he paralleled human behavior. Page 86.

wit: the power of thinking and reasoning rationally; mental soundness or sanity; understanding. Page 18.

witness, bear false: to tell lies or state something false while under oath or in a court of law; to state falsely. *Bear* means to give or provide. *Witness* means swearing to a fact, statement, etc.; proof or evidence. Page 88.

wit, to: used to introduce a list or explanation of what one has just mentioned. Originally a phrase used in law, *that is to wit,* which meant that is to know, that is to say. Page 34.

workaday: pertaining to or characteristic of a workday and its occupations. Page 9.

working over: an examination or study of something that is done thoroughly and in detail. Page 21.

wormed (one's) way into: maneuvered (oneself) gradually into an area or position by devious or subtle means. Page 72.

wrested: gained with difficulty by or as if by force. Page 30.

wretch: an unfortunate or unhappy person. Page 13.

wrought: an older form of *worked,* put together, created or fashioned in a skillful way. Page 7.

Wundt: Wilhelm Wundt (1832–1920), German psychologist and physiologist; the originator of modern psychology and the false doctrine that Man is no more than an animal. Page 67.

Y

yardstick: a standard used to judge the quality, value or success of something. Page 59.

yarn: an entertaining story of real or fictitious adventures. Page 8.

YP: a designation for *yard patrol,* in reference to a patrol vessel, such as one assigned to escort ships in a harbor or local area. Page 11.

INDEX

Burks, Arthur J.

tour of Sing Sing with L. Ron Hubbard, 8

C

capital punishment, 15

car

borrowed boots returned in a stolen car, 7

caved in

definition, 60

C.C.C., 24

cell

womb and, 18

Central Division

Los Angeles, 12

Chart of Human Evaluation, 31

Chefoo

justice and, 30

children, rearing of, 50

China, 30

execution witnessed in, 30

justice procedures observed, 30

Chinese "Conservatism," 30

Chinese "Liberalism," 30

chromosomal violence tendency, 3

church attendance

diminished, proliferation of pornography and, 86

Civilian Conservation Corps, 24

Clouston, D. M.

letter to L. Ron Hubbard on insanity defense and, 74

reply from L. Ron Hubbard to, 75

Colombia

The Way to Happiness and, 104–105

come to grief, 63

communication

dynamics in, 61

dynamics out of, example, 62–64

Communist

"justice" and, 41

conditions

formulas to better, 33

Conditions of Existence, 1

conduct

destruction, fear and unethical, 57

morals and code of good, 59

survival and ethical, 56

Congo

The Way to Happiness and, 106

Constitution

justice written into, 37

Penal Code and, 45

construction

destruction and, 56

correctional facility

oxymoron, 35

courts

liable to act on false reports, 41

coward

inevitably a liar, 57

crime

accidental and intentional, 77

committing the first, 21

definition, 59

drug related, rise in, 85

lawless and irresponsible public attitude toward, 69, 71

psychiatry and, 71–72

psychiatry, psychology and the precipitation of, 67

punishment and, 7, 9

psychiatry and, 67–69

"Criminal College, The," 17–24

criminality

definition, 76

illiteracy and, 86, 109

past forms of punishment and, 78

God Dynamic, 51

good, 31–32, 56

gradient, 51

Group Dynamic, 50

Infinity Dynamic, 51

insanity as defined by law, 76

logic, 53

Mankind Dynamic, 50

MEST, 50

morals, 59

optimum solution, 53

out-ethics, 53

physical universe, 50

Second Dynamic, 50

Self Dynamic, 50

Seventh Dynamic, 51

Sex Dynamic, 50

Sixth Dynamic, 50

Spiritual Dynamic, 51

Third Dynamic, 50

Universe Dynamic, 50

degradation, 57

way out of, 61

delinquency

common denominator of, 14

democracy

breakdown of Western, 41

destruction

construction and, 56

"Deterioration of Liberty, The"

lecture, 117

Dianetics, 11

Dianetics and Scientology

L. Ron Hubbard, Founder, 1

Dianetics: The Modern Science of Mental Health

Bay Head, New Jersey and, 15

discipline

criminal and, 23

dishonesty, 57

divorce rates

increase of, 85

"Donald Duck" navy, 10

drug rehabilitation program

world's most successful, 86

drugs, 56

addiction to alcohol or, 63

teenager taking, 61

testing with prisoners, 68

drunks

LRH handlings of intoxicated men, 13

dwindling spiral

ethics and, 53

Dynamic Principle of Existence, 49, 54

dynamics, 49–51

comprising life, 61

concentric circles, series of, 51

definition, 50

eight, 49

Eighth, 51

ethics, justice and, 48–63

Fifth, 50

First, 50, 51, 56, 61, 63

Fourth, 50

future and, 56

groups, 50

in communication and, 61

listed, 51

optimum solution and, 53

out-ethics, 61–63

and consequences on other, 62

Second Dynamic and, 63

out of communication, 59

examples, 62–64

relative importance between, 50, 51

Second, 50, 54, 61, 63

Seventh, 51

Sixth, 50

stressing one or a combination more than others, 50

Third, 50, 51, 61

victim of one's, 60

dynamics of human existence

survival and, 31

E

education

via the prison system, 23

eight dynamics

see **dynamics**

Eighth Dynamic

definition, 51

discovering the true, 51

electric chair, 8

electroshock

prisoners tested with, 68

England

prison colony system, 23

Eoanthropic chieftain, 17

ethics, 53–54

application, 1

definition, 1, 8, 31

dynamics and, 49–63

for the individual, 53

in-ethics

see **in-ethics**

interaction with other dynamics, 61

justice and, 29–35

dynamics and, 49–63

failure to apply, 59

your survival, 60–61

justice as substitute, 60

long-term survival concepts and, 53

Man can learn how to put in his own, 35

optimum survival and, 54

out-ethics

see **out-ethics**

past traditional aims of, 35

rationality and, 53

right and wrong conduct, 56

"Ethics, Justice and the Dynamics," 48–63

Ethics Technology, 1

rehabilitation and, 33, 86

evil

conduct, 56

definition, 32, 56

good and, 54–57

intentions, person seeks to suppress
  them, 54

non-survival conduct, 56

pain and, 53

evolutionary psychology, 86, 87

"Excalibur," 8, 9, 29

executioner

person becoming his own, 54

F

fair hearing, 45

fair trial, 45

false accusations

basic breakdown of justice and, 41

false reports

breaking down

nation's structure, 41

Western democracy, 41

family, 50

fear

destructive acts and, 57

unethical conduct and, 57

Fifth Dynamic

definition, 50

Filipino

injustice and, 37

First Dynamic, 51

dead and most wrong on, 56

definition, 50

man stealing from employer and, 61

unhappiness on, 63

I

ideals
    survival and, 59

illegitimate births, 85

illiteracy
    criminality and, 86, 109

illness
    developing incapacitating, 54

immortality, 53, 54

indecision
    Graph of Logic and, 53

Indonesia
    Criminon results in, 111
    National Criminon Center, 111

in-ethics
    dynamics and, 62
    see also **ethics**

infanticide, 54

infinity, 51
    entirely right and, 56

Infinity Dynamic
    definition, 51

infinity symbol, 51

influence
    zero of, 60

injustice
    bulk of American riots and, 37
    revolution and, 37

insanity, 57
    criminal and, 79
    definition, 76
    jail sentences and, 79
    permitting criminals to escape law by
        reason of, 78
    prohibited as a defense, 79

insanity defense
    criminals and, 78
    D. M. Clouston letter to LRH on, 74

insecurity
    personal, 42

intentions
    evil, seeking to suppress one's, 54
    Man and basic, 54

Introduction to Scientology Ethics, 35
    photograph, 34

**I will not admit that there is a naturally
    bad...,** 1, 117

J

jail sentences
    insanity and, 79

Japanese
    judicial procedures observed, 30

job
    satisfaction of well done, 62

Joliet, Illinois
    state penitentiary, 7

"Ju Chia," 30

jurisprudence
    breakthrough in the field of, 41

justice, 41–43
    basic breakdown of, 41
    dynamics and, 49–63
    ethics and, 29–35
        dynamics and, 49–63
        failure to apply, and, 59
        trying to substitute for, 60
        your survival and, 60–61
    L. Ron Hubbard's justice system, 34
    not affordable by all, riots and, 37
    past traditional aims of, 35
    protection of the innocent and decent, 60
    Scientology system of, 35
    used until, 60
    Western powers pulling up honor and, 43
    when used and not used, 61

K

killer apes in the fast lane, 68

King, Rodney
distribution of "Riots" and, 36

knowledge
of ethics, 61

L

LAPD
Special Officer, 2, 12

laws
of universe, 59
purpose and function of, 80

liar
cutting own throat, 61
inevitably a coward, 57

lies
why they are told, 57

life
divisions of, 49
group effort, 61
highly productive, 57
state and, 44

logic
definition, 53
graph of, 52–53

long-term survival concepts, 53

Los Angeles, California
Central Division, 12
City Hall, photograph, 13
The Way to Happiness and, 104, 112

Los Angeles detention center
The Way to Happiness, results in using, 111

Los Angeles Police Department
Special Officer, 2, 12

love, 57

loyalty
disruption of, 41

M

Maine
Portsmouth Naval Prison, crew on
ship, 10

Man
basically good, 11, 32, 54, 61
greatest weapon, 53
I will not admit that there is a naturally
bad..., 117
"justice" cannot be trusted in hands of, 60
push-button stimulus-response robot, 71,
73
seeking survival, 62

"Man-from-mud," 86

Manhattan
impressions of, circa 1973, 85
sociological studies, 2

Man is an animal theory, 67, 71

Man is basically good, 11, 32, 54, 61

Mankind Dynamic
definition, 50

MEST
definition, 50

Metropolitan Detective Agency, 12

Mexico
Criminon, drop in recidivism rate, 111

minority groups
injustice and, 42

moral codes
abandoning, 63
group wishing to practice license
against, 59
origin of, 59
The Way to Happiness
book on film, 99
nonreligious, common sense, 88
photographs, 84, 98

morals, 57–59
definition, 59

survival, measured in, 62

Poland

The Way to Happiness and, 112

politicians

psychiatrists and psychologists and, 71

pornography

diminished church attendance and
proliferation of, 86

Portsmouth Naval Prison, Maine

L. Ron Hubbard's crew and, 10

photograph, 10

Princeton University

photograph, 29

United States Naval School of Military
Government, 29

prison colony system, 23

one prison colony which did survive, 23

prisoners

guinea pigs for testing

drugs, 68

electroshock, 68

psychosurgical experimentation, 68

parole system and release of, 79

prison (system), 2, 17

Criminon program and, 109–113

revolving door, 16

sentencing of a man to prison, return to
womb and, 17

problem

resolution, 51

professor of hooeyology, 21

psychologists/psychiatrists

corrupt pressure groups, 41

crimes, 71

psychotropic drugs and, 68

rehabilitative programs attempted, 68

psychology/psychiatry

crime and, 71–72

crime and punishment and, 67–69

easy seizure and, 42

psychosurgical experimentation

prisoners tested with, 68

punishment, 44

capital, 15

courts and, 35

crime and, 7, 9

psychiatry and, 67–69

effect of punishment on a criminal, 16

insanity and, 79

escaping, 78

no ethics, self-punishment and, 61

past forms and criminality and, 78

rehabilitation instead of, 33

religion not influential and, 86

revenge and, 79

R

race, 50

rationality

toward the highest level of survival, 53

reason, 53

moral codes and absence of extended, 59

ultimate in, 59

recidivism, 16

Criminon and lowered, 110

drop in rate of, 111

stiff penalties and, 34

reform school, 21

rehabilitation

Ethics Technology and, 33

Group Processing of criminals, 80

instead of punishment, 33

psychology and psychiatry failures, 68

The Way to Happiness and, 109

religion

morality and the state and, 86

revolution

injustice, suppressed wrath and, 37

mechanics of, 42

THE
L. RON HUBBARD
SERIES

"To really know life," L. Ron Hubbard wrote, "you've got to be part of life. You must get down and look, you must get into the nooks and crannies of existence. You have to rub elbows with all kinds and types of men before you can finally establish what he is."

Through his long and extraordinary journey to the founding of Dianetics and Scientology, Ron did just that. From his adventurous youth in a rough and tumble American West to his far-flung trek across a still mysterious Asia; from his two-decade search for the very essence of life to the triumph of Dianetics and Scientology—such are the stories recounted in the L. Ron Hubbard Biographical Publications.

Drawn from his own archival collection, this is Ron's life as he himself saw it. With each volume of the series focusing upon a separate field of endeavor, here are the compelling facts, figures, anecdotes and photographs from a life like no other.

Indeed, here is the life of a man who lived at least twenty lives in the space of one.

FOR FURTHER INFORMATION VISIT
www.lronhubbard.org

The L. Ron Hubbard Series
A PROFILE

To order copies of *The L. Ron Hubbard Series*
or L. Ron Hubbard's Dianetics and
Scientology books and lectures, contact:

US AND INTERNATIONAL

BRIDGE PUBLICATIONS, INC.
5600 E. Olympic Blvd.
Commerce, California 90022 USA
www.bridgepub.com
Tel: (323) 888-6200
Toll-free: 1-800-722-1733

UNITED KINGDOM AND EUROPE

NEW ERA PUBLICATIONS
INTERNATIONAL ApS
Smedeland 20
2600 Glostrup, Denmark
www.newerapublications.com
Tel: (45) 33 73 66 66
Toll-free: 00-800-808-8-8008